MIL-TECH SERIES

THE
WILD WEASELS

History of US Air Force SAM Killers, 1965 to Today

D1476961

Hans Halberstadt

To Bronwyn, for everything.

First published in 1992 by Motorbooks International Publishers & Wholesalers, PO Box 2, 729 Prospect Avenue, Osceola, WI 54020 USA

Motorbooks International books are also available at discounts in bulk quantity for industrial or sales-promotional use. For details write to Special Sales Manager at the Publisher's address

Library of Congress Cataloging-in-Publication Data
    Halberstadt, Hans.
        The Wild Weasels / Hans Halberstadt.
            p.   cm.—(Motorbooks International mil-tech series)
        Includes index.
        ISBN 0-87938-662-2
        1. Electronic warfare aircraft.   I.
    Title.   II. Series.
    UG1242.E43H35   1992
    358.4′5—dc20   92-28519

On the front cover: An F-4G Wild Weasel Phantom slides up to the tanker for fuel.

On the back cover: Top, two fully loaded F-4Gs waddle out to the runway for another mission during Operation Desert Storm. Center, two-seat F-105F Thunderchiefs were converted into the first truly effective Wild Weasel aircraft. Bottom, the first Wild Weasel aircraft were built on the two-seat F-100F airframe. *USAF photos via Bob Dorr*

Printed and bound in the United States of America

Contents

Acknowledgments

Special thanks to those pioneer Weasels who helped with this project: Tom Wilson, Chuck Horner, Mike Gilroy, Billy Sparks, and Jack Donovan, for their humor and insights, and for their courage long ago and far away.

Thanks also to today's crop of Weasels, especially Lieutenant Colonel Ron Barrett, Lieutenant Colonel John ("John Boy") Walton, Captain Gil Zamora, Colonel Ray Karp, and Colonel Patton at George Air Force Base, California. And a sincere salute to Captain Jim Tynan and his staff of "high-speed, low-drag" public affairs troops.

Preface

Books about systems and missions like those of the Wild Weasel community are something of a challenge to write—and sometimes to read, as well. That's because the information about these systems almost always starts out in some secret or top secret program. Sooner or later parts of the program become public, but usually in fragmentary ways, and normally many years after a system has entered service. That's certainly the case with the Wild Weasel, an essential, successful, and extremely interesting part of the US Air Force.

Even the photographs presented here of Phantom's rear cockpit were made only after a lot of thoughtful review and debate and a few calls to senior U.S. Air Force security officers. The data about the receiver in that cockpit, the APR-47 Radar Attack and Warning Receiver, the missile that it works with, the High-Speed Anti-Radiation Missile (HARM), and even the old Phantom itself are sensitive and closely held. And accounts of how missions were flown, even back twenty-five years ago, are still somewhat restricted. That makes telling a complete and accurate story something of a tactical problem.

Even so, the Air Force was extremely forthcoming with hard data for this report. The pictures of the APR-47 are among the only ones ever permitted. And some of the accounts of how Weasels fly and fight include information that has only recently been declassified. Although it limits the amount of information that is available, I still believe we must respect the need of the Air Force to protect itself through this security classification system, and I have made no attempt to evade it.

Another, related part of the problem with these books is that a lot of the data that is presented in books and magazines just doesn't agree with the data published on the same systems in other books and magazines. We all want to tell a complete and detailed story about these men and missiles, even without reliable data, which is why the AGM-45 Shrike missile is variously described as having a three-plus mile range in one publication and a ten-plus mile range in another. Which one is right? Give us a missile to test and we'll find out.

And, yet another caution: even accurate specifications can lie. An airplane whose published maximum speed is (for example) Mach 1.5 will almost never break the sound barrier in the real world. That's because those specifications are written normally for the testing ranges, not hostile airspace where bombs and missiles and drop tanks hang from the wings. About the only way to really evaluate airplanes is to load them up with bombs, rockets, missiles and crews and turn them loose on each other in combat. Not training combat, even at its most realistic, but the real world where losers learn their lessons from the inside of a fireball or under a canopy. So, be careful reading data in books about military aircraft—including this one.

I know a little about air combat in the real world, having flown 127 missions in Vietnam, mostly in helicopters as a door gunner, but a couple in fighters, just for fun. Not one of my missions—not all 127 of them stacked end to end—were as dangerous, as important, or as demanding as any single one flown by my helpers on this book: Tom Wilson (Lieutenant Colonel, U.S. Air Force Ret.), Mike Gilroy (Colonel, U.S. Air Force Ret.), Billy Sparks (Lieutenant Colonel, U.S. Air Force Ret.), Jack Donovan (Lieutenant Colonel, U.S. Air Force Ret.), and Chuck Horner, (General, U.S. Air Force). We all owe these guys, and the others, living and dead, a salute (and a beer) for their incredible courage over North Vietnam a long time ago. The success of Desert Storm's air defense suppression campaign was built on the missions these incredible men flew back then, the losses they took and the lessons they learned. These men were among the greatest heroes of the air war over North Vietnam, are all heavily decorated, and all offered extensive support for this book. Their recollections and insights are more valuable than a bucket of statistics.

Chapter 1

Mission Brief

It began the way these things usually begin—with a learning experience. The year was 1965, the place was the air space of North Vietnam. One of the largest, most developed nations of the world (the United States) was involved in a war with one of the smallest and most backward (North Vietnam). And much to the surprise of everyone involved, the former was taking some hard licks from the latter.

Carrier attack aircraft were flying from the *Constellation* and *Ticonderoga* in the Tonkin Gulf, and Air Force fighters and bombers were operating from bases in South Vietnam and Thailand against targets in North Vietnam. But they were

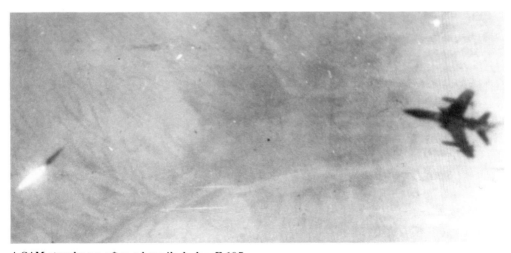

A SAM streaks up after a heavily laden F-105 Thunderchief, or "Thud," somewhere over North Vietnam. USAF photo via Mike Gilroy

An F-100F Super Sabre, or "Hun," unglues from the deck, off in search of adventure. Seven of these aircraft were tasked with the original mission, loaded with the best technology that 1965 money could buy, and sent off to defeat the evil horde. They did, too, at a cost of about half the aircraft, which were lost or damaged beyond repair in combat, the rest being bent beyond salvation. USAF via Bob Dorr

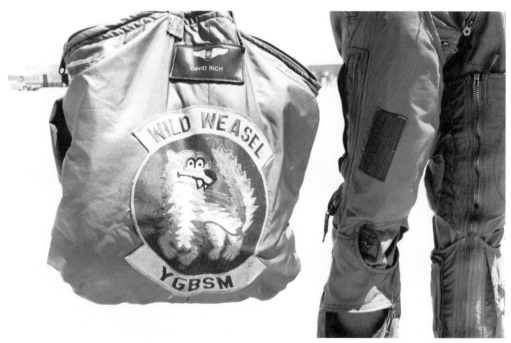

It's been a long time since a young Captain Jack Donovan stood up to utter those immortal words, but they're still part of the legend and lore of the Wild Weasel—witness the semiofficial emblem of the breed: a bewildered little critter with the tastefully abbreviated battle cry first uttered by Donovan: "You gotta be shitting me!"

discovering (the hard way) that it wasn't quite as easy as everybody expected. Guns of many calibers and missiles of several kinds were well deployed around strategic targets along the coast and near the major cities. They flew A-4 Skyhawks, A-1 Skyraiders, A-7 Crusaders, and F-4 Phantoms on missions code named Pierce Arrow, hitting naval installations, fuel storage facilities, rail yards, and port facilities.

Despite what the newspapers were reporting back home, attacks were not going very well. The strikes were running into some really heavy air defenses, and the defenses used effective systems for low, medium, and high altitudes, all integrated and coordinated from the ground. Aircraft were getting hit, and a lot were being lost. The strikes were intended to teach the North Vietnamese communists that there would be a high price to pay for

a conflict with the United States. But the lesson *actually* taught was that aircraft were highly vulnerable to all sorts of weapons, and that the actual application of combat power against the strategic sites in North Vietnam was too costly to sustain for very long without some way to counter the defenses. And the defenses turned out to be far more sophisticated and elaborate than anyone—except perhaps the defenders—had imagined.

The problem was rapidly identified. The North Vietnamese had been well supplied, in secret, by the Soviet Union with a full spectrum of antiaircraft weapons of modern design, along with the command and control systems needed to make these weapons effective. Now, if the Soviets do anything well, it is the design of weapons and the doctrine to employ them. Their idea is to make systems that are simple, durable, and reasonably effec-

A brace of G-model Thuds take a break from the festivities and take on gas from a KC-135 tanker over Vietnam. USAF via Bob Dorr

tive and to produce them in tremendous volume. They don't care whether or not a weapon uses the latest technology as long as it works and there are lots of them. Still the Soviets don't ignore advanced technology, either, when it works, and they had come up with some very good, very advanced systems that worked exactly as advertised.

The Soviets started supplying the North Vietnamese with batteries of huge SA-2 Guideline surface-to-air missiles (SAMs) that were guided by ground operators using a radar system the North Atlantic Treaty Organization (NATO) code named Fansong. The missiles traveled at about three times the speed of sound, were highly accurate and extremely difficult to avoid. These missile batteries were linked and commanded by a sophisticated command and control network that pro-

During one daylight attack on a SAM site, an intrepid participant of Bobbin flight recorded these hits and secondary explosions caused by direct hits on the radar van, 20mm cannon fire across the site, and twelve bombs on the revetments. USAF photo via Mike Gilroy

vided early warning and tactical coordination. They worked best at the medium altitudes where the American attackers thought they'd be safe from the many 37mm and 57mm guns. The big SAM was guided from the ground, with amazing accuracy. The only real way to avoid one was to jettison all the bombs and tanks on the hard-points and maneuver like hell in the faint, fond hope of outturning it. However the missile threat was so unexpected at first that the strike aircraft didn't even try to evade the SAMs, and instead would get nailed while motoring along straight and level.

One of the awful frustrations for the U.S. Air Force pilots conducting operations against North Vietnam was that the missiles were, at one point, easy targets and highly vulnerable, and yet they were protected by—of all people—the U.S. government. The SAMs arrived on the decks of Russian ships and were often photographed en route. The recon planes could see them on the docks in Haiphong, coming off the ships and onto trucks and trains. But the rules of engagement of the time forbade attacks against them there, out in the open, lest the Soviets be antagonized. So the Air Force, Navy, and Marine pilots had to wait until the systems were in place and operational before engaging them, and for many Americans that was simply too late.

The SAMs were first used in June of 1965. American pilots quickly began calling the SA-2 the "flying telephone pole." An F-4C was the first to fall to the missile, in July, and others quickly followed. A lot of aircraft were quickly lost to the SAMs; for one short period, the North Vietnamese were downing an airplane with every SAM launched. As one of the crews of that era recalls, "There was a lot of talk, in and out of the Pentagon, that airplanes just can't survive up here. And if you were up there, boy, you *knew* it! It was the age of the missile, and there seemed no way to survive over there. You can't go low, because of the flak; can't go high because you can't see the target; now you can't go medium altitude because the SAM will kill you!"

The missiles forced the American strikers down from the higher altitudes, where the SAMs were most effective and difficult to avoid, and right into the effective ranges of another part of the Soviet-designed system, a network of antiaircraft artillery (AAA, or "triple-A") of several calibers and types. This was quite a surprise because American planners had pretty much dismissed triple-A as an old, obsolete, insignificant threat. The pilots had other ideas about it, particularly when it was making holes in their airplanes.

The triple-A was also tied into the command and control net and some systems were radar aimed. So the air crews that launched from the carriers *Ranger* and *Enterprise* in the Gulf of Tonkin found themselves flying into a cloud of flying steel down low, Mach two SAMs up high, plus MiGs in the clouds, and small arms fire down on the deck . . . none of which helped the accuracy of their ordnance delivery. It was, indeed, quite a learning experience.

The Birth of the Wild Weasel

The initial euphoria of the air crews who flew the first missions was replaced by both dread and the realization that something had to be done to deal with the threat of this multilayered air defense system. The planners desperately started designing missions to attack the air defense systems and dedicated some of their assets to this specialized role.

The introduction of the SAMs and the sudden turn of fate for the air war produced a frantic development effort back in the States. A coalition of manufacturers

Half of a SAM site is neatly enveloped by the effects of dozens of explosions. The CBU (cluster bomb unit) is and was a great weapon. But if it goes off too high above the ground the result is an embarrassing ring around the target, with the intended victim untouched. USAF via Tom Wilson

and military organizations was assembled, given a top priority for resources, and ordered to come up with a solution. Part of this coalition came from a small electronics company in Palo Alto, California, Applied Technology. Two of their engineers had been walking the corridors of the Pentagon, trying to interest the Air Force in their newly developed radio frequency (RF) receiver/direction finder —without much luck. But with the threat of the SAM's radar component, somebody realized the engineers' system might be part of the solution.

A small task force of contractors and Air Force project officers met in a confer-

Mike Gilroy has a right to grin; 100 missions are more than a whole lifetime for many Thud drivers. Gilroy retired as a colonel, a pioneer, and the namesake of the Gilroy trophy, *awarded to the winner of the annual electronic warfare competition at Nellis Air Force Base.* Mike Gilroy

ence room and brainstormed the problem and possible solution. A contract was sketched out on a blackboard and photographed for the record. On the basis of this record and a handshake, work began. It was that kind of problem.

A platform for the system was required. It needed to be reasonably fast and have two seats and room for the various black boxes, plus hard points for bombs, rockets, and guns. The F-100F Super Sabre was chosen. It was not entirely perfect, but it was available.

The Thud is an airplane much beloved by many of its crews, a strong, fast, reliable survivor. This one is tricked out with auxiliary fuel tanks, an ARC-380 ECM (electronic countermeasures) pod on the fuselage and Shrikes on the pylons. USAF photo via Bob Dorr

Another F-105, this one with AGM-78B Standard ARM (Anti-Radiation Missile) missiles in addition to the Shrikes. USAF photo via Bob Dorr

AGM-45 Shrike Missile

At the same time, a frantic development project was underway to design, test, produce, and field an anti-radiation missile—one that would reliably and effectively home on a radar emitter and destroy it. That effort produced the AGM-45 Shrike. The Shrike had its limitations—and still has them because it is still in service—but it performed as advertised. Each Shrike only works against a portion of the radar frequency spectrum, so you've got to have the right model slung under the wing to do any good. But the missile allowed, for the first time, the comparative safety of a few miles stand-off range for the SAM hunter. Suddenly, North Vietnamese radar operators found their antennas—and often themselves—effectively targeted by aircraft that never came in gun or missile range. The learning experience worked both ways.

Wild Weasel Crews

The crews selected for the mission were among the best in the Air Force—but nobody told them what they were going to be doing until it was, in effect, too late. The pilots were relatively easy to find: they had to be superb "sticks" with most of their lifetime in fighters. The electronic warfare officers, EWOs or "Bears" (short for "trained bears") as they would soon be called, were a different story—there was no such animal at the time. Navigators were selected for the job and sent off on their secret mission.

The pilots and navigators were assembled in a briefing room. A succession

AGM-45 Shrike mounted on an F-4. USAF photo via Bob Dorr

of officers briefed them on their new assignment and described the threat and the mission to defeat it. In enthusiastic terms, the operations officers explained that all the F-100F pilots had to do was to fly around over enemy territory until the new radar warning receiver indicated they were being illuminated by the threat radars of the missile or gun systems. The F-100F's new (then) state-of-the-art radar warning receiver could then indicate a bearing on the threat, which would let the pilot fly directly toward it. Once over the top, the pilot should be able to see the gun or missile battery—or at least their output—which would clearly identify the target to the cunning attackers. The F-100F pilots would then come back around to drop bombs on the positions and then go home.

Of course, the operations officers said, there were a few problems with the mission: the radar warning receivers only offered bearing information, not range, which made target identification rather awkward. Then there was the problem of the target itself, which would naturally resent the attentions of the aircraft and would shoot at it with everything available. Then, too, there was the problem of target engagement; iron bombs are notoriously inaccurate, and when the aircraft that is dropping them is getting shot at by an accurate system, the bomber's accuracy doesn't improve at all. But, said the briefer, it was an important mission and *somebody* had to do it. Any questions?

There was silence in the room for a few moments, then Captain Jack Donovan got to his feet. What he said wasn't a question, really, but a comment that has been preserved through the decades as part of the lore of the Wild Weasel. Donovan looked at the briefing officer, who had just described what amounted to a suicide mission, and said with sincere disgust, "You gotta be shitting me!"

Well, the briefers weren't. The navigators were paired with pilots, hastily trained, and shipped off to the tropical climes. The F-100Fs started flying the missions, and just as the young EWO suspected, the airplanes and their crews started falling out of the skies. The F-100F, the rudimentary tactics, and the prototype equipment in the little black boxes were not equal to the task, and the crews paid the price. Of the seven aircraft sent over, two were quickly shot down, another was bent beyond repair, and all were damaged to the point of uselessness.

There is still a scrapbook in the Wild Weasel training squadron at George Air Force Base with the pictures of graduates from the program of those days. Along with the clippings and articles are the class portraits from that time. Next to many of the smiling young faces are the notations "KIA, 1965" (for "killed in action") or "POW, 1966."

But the attacks—however costly—proved some things: at least seven SAM sites were destroyed in exchange for their own losses. This success against the SAMs started to have the desired effect on the amount of scrap metal flying through the North's air space. The enemy radar operators learned a new lesson: they could no longer operate with impunity, and some of them started to die.

The first kill came on 22 December 1965. In their F-100F, Captain Al Lamb and Captain Jack Donovan led a flight of four F-105 Thuds. All the aircraft carried four rocket pods, each with twenty-four 2.75-inch, high-explosive, unguided rockets. The F-100F was to be the "hunter" that would find the site, and the Thuds were to be the "killers" that would lay the heavy metal on the target.

"I detected a signal," Jack Donovan recalls, "a strong signal from what must have been the dumbest SAM site in the world because he stayed up continuously for the next twelve minutes." They descend from 12,000 feet, with Al Lamb flying a series of "dog-legs" in order to give Donovan a way to establish the position of the site by a sequence of lines-of-bearing. Lamb and Donovan feel their way across the terrain, using the systems to try to find the emitter. Lamb pops over a ridge, turns hard, and follows the valley, then turns hard again, with a little parade of Thuds in trail. "There we were, right in the guy's back door," Donovan says.

"He's right there, on the left!" Donovan calls, and Lamb sees the site under its camouflage. Two hundred feet above the terrain, Lamb hauls back on the stick and pulls up steeply to begin his attack—

a pop-up and turn back on the target—almost running out of airspeed at the top. The Thuds fan out astern, unable to maintain formation during the attack maneuvering. Lamb unloads two cans of rockets, a total of forty-eight, centered on the radar van. The lead Thud driver now sees the target, yells "I've got it, I've got it!" and leads the four F-105 killers in to blanket the site with their rockets.

While the Thuds are busy lightening their aircraft, Donovan watches another site come up on his scope. "Now guns!" yells Lamb, and the flight shoots up the place until the barrels melt. Then the flight begins to egress, making as clean a getaway as the local authorities will permit

The Wild Weasel class that arrived at Takhli Royal Thailand Air Force Base on 4 July 1966 with seven airplanes. By 11 August all aircraft had been shot down. Four of the class would finish 100 missions, four were killed in action, two became POWs, two were wounded in action, and four failed to finish their tours for various reasons. USAF photo via Mike Gilroy

(giggling like teenagers, according to Donovan). They take on fuel from a tanker and overfly their Korat base in a V-for-victory formation.

The success of the mission validated the basic idea and the basic hardware and pointed the way toward effective tactics. The effectiveness of the strike and the ones that followed did more than just suppress individual sites, it inhibited the whole enemy air defense system. As a result, the American strikes against strategic North Vietnamese targets became more effective and less dangerous.

But the bottom line was still not acceptable. The F-100F was just not equal to the task and was quickly replaced by the F-105F Thunderchief in 1966 and later the improved F-105G in 1968. The "Thud" wasn't as maneuverable as the old F-100, but it was faster and had longer range and better avionics. It was the first aircraft able to launch the AGM-45 Shrike and AGM-78 Standard Anti-Radiation Missiles. Best of all, it was armored!

Despite the kidding of the Phantom and Skyhawk drivers at the bar about the name of the airplane ("What's the sound of an F-105 hitting the ground? THUD!"), it was a survivable airframe that could take plenty of hits before coming apart. And F-105s took lots of hits over the next few years, soldiering on to the end of the war, and beyond.

The F-4C Phantom joined the Thud in the Wild Weasel mission three years later, in 1969, but the F-105 continued to serve throughout the rest of the war. The F-4C was supposed to be an improvement on the F-105F but more was needed, and an improved model version of the Phantom was designed around the highly sophisticated APR-38 Radar Attack and Warning receiver (upgraded to the APR-47 in 1990–91). The new aircraft was designated the F-4G and still serves today.

The mission needed a name, and originally it was going to be "Wild Ferret," but that name had been used in Korea. So instead, the code name selected was "Wild Weasel," a reference to the little creature with sharp teeth who brazenly goes into the burrows of much larger, more powerful enemies and kills them. The weasel is a rather cute little guy, fearless and energetic, and he gets the job done. Even so, weasels get hurt sometimes, and sometimes even the brave little weasel must have second thoughts about the enemies he has to confront. So, when it came time to create an emblem for the Wild Weasels, the design included an image of a little weasel, with a slightly distressed expression, surrounded by the acronym for that very first weasel EWO's words back in the very first briefing: YGBSM.

After the Wild Weasel program started showing promise, the Air Force rapidly developed the program under conditions of extremely high priority. For the crews, the experience could be an adventure in all sorts of ways. Lieutenant General Chuck Horner was a captain then, a Thud driver, and one of the early pilots recruited for the mission. He recalls something of the urgency of the time, how be became a Wild Weasel "stick," and how he and his Bear got "married":

"I was an instructor at Nellis and was trying to get back over to Vietnam. They were looking for guys with fighter experience. One morning I was out at Mobile Control, watching students trying to land and take off; Al Lamb was there, and I mentioned to him that I was trying to get back. 'Do you want to go over as a Weasel?' Lamb asked. 'Sure,' I told him. That was at 7:30 in the morning. At 11:00 I had orders.

"We reported to the squadron. So they had these pilots and the EWOs—the electronic warfare officers—and they had a 'social' the first night. You were supposed to pair up, kind of like 'The Dating Game.' Well, Billy Sparks and I were bound and determined that we weren't going to play any games. So we waited around and got the last two EWOs. The choice was sort of forced on us, but it worked out fine."

Tom Wilson is now a retired Air Force colonel and successful novelist (*Termite Hill* and other stories about the air war over the North), but over North Vietnam he was known as one of the best Bears in the business. He'd been one of the early navigators tapped for the mission, and he remembers it from the EWO perspective:

"We went to Nellis and were accelerated through a perfunctory course of quickie classroom training and ten Thud rides while the airplanes were being prepared, then we flew our airplanes over. The reason? All of the airplanes at Takhli, our destination, had been shot down or so badly damaged that they were basket cases.

"When Jerry Hoblit and I arrived at Takhli, the shootdown rate was more than sixty percent. Less than forty percent were completing their hundred missions. But the shootdown rate for the Weasels was even higher; the first group lost all their airplanes and most of their crews.

"When we arrived there were no real tactics developed for the Weasels yet. We were supposed to escort the strike force, protect them from the SAMs, but they didn't say how. It was a learn-as-you-go process and we all made a lot of mistakes. I knew a little about how to operate the equipment, and Jerry knew how to drop CBU-24s and bombs, and a bit about how to fire the Shrike missile (he'd never fired one) but that was about it. Our first time as Weasel flight lead was *awful*. We crossed the Red River in the weather; SAMs were fired at us from under the cloud cover. How do you see them? So we

started looking for these 'flying telephone poles' we'd heard about—but the first one didn't look like that at all as it came zipping out of a cloud. At Mach 3 it was just a streak and a bang! It went off right under our airplane. We thought we'd been shot down! We were flailing around the sky, trying to recover, to find out how bad it was . . .and I heard Jerry say, 'Are you okay?' And I was checking myself out, looking for wounds—but not finding any—so I said, 'Uh . . . yeah.' So we collected our flight, regrouped, and went on to attack the target. We'd learned some things, dodged a few SAMs; we were there to protect the flight from SAMs—to kill SAM sites—but we were having a tough time just protecting ourselves. So Jerry and I went back and we studied and worked and by the time we left we killed a *lot* of them! It wasn't like it grew to be, when you claimed a kill if you launched an itsy missile at it. We didn't claim a SAM site kill unless we bombed it out of existence. But I've got to admit, it didn't start very gloriously.

"At one point in early 1967 Takhli was down to about seven or eight Wild Weasel crews, and they were likely the most highly decorated of that war. Out of that number there were awarded two Medals of Honor, three or four Air Force Crosses, dozens of Silver Stars, and scores of Distinguished Flying Crosses—and, like my friend Mike Gilroy says, too many Purple Hearts. Most of the men were either killed in action or spent the next seven years as POWs. When we got there no one survived; by the time we left everyone was getting a lot smarter with their tactics. Billy Sparks and his Bear, Carlo, arrived the day I left. Later he told me that during his entire tour not a single crew was lost on a Wild Weasel mission. Billy was later shot down while flying a strike mission."

Thud drivers often sneer at the Phantom, the airframe that supplemented rather than replaced the F-105 in Vietnam. The Phantom was supposed to do everything for everybody: fighter, bomber, close air support.

Initially the missions are based on flights of four, but the crews quickly discover that, down low, twisting and turning, the number three and number four aircraft can't easily keep up. So they break into two-ship formations, a Weasel to be the hunter and a wingman with pig iron to be the killer. The Weasel flights go in first, twenty miles ahead of the strike package, one flight on each side of the flight corridor. They already know approximately where the sites are. Once in the area the Weasels throttle back, teasing the operators to shoot—and exposing themselves in the process. The two flights provide mutual support; when one Weasel is engaged by a site, the other attacks the site while the first evades the missile. "It worked," says one of the EWOs. "We were killing a site every day!"

By the time American involvement in the war concluded, the business of defense suppression had been raised to an art form. There were still losses, as there will always be. But the Weasel mission— with stand-off anti-radiation missiles and pilots and EWOs with experience and courage—turned the tables on North Vietnam. It was and is a team sport. As Tom Wilson says, "Without the highly experienced pilot, you won't survive or kill anything. Without the highly trained EWO, you won't find anything to kill."

When the bombing missions were halted, it was not because of combat losses in the skies over Hanoi and Haiphong, but because of political losses at home. Strike packages were able to hit targets effectively and with acceptable losses, despite the guns and the missiles. On the ground, radar operators had to be handcuffed to their consoles to keep them operating because of the threat from the Wild Weasels.

The system worked so well that there were no real changes from the early 1970s until the early 1990s. The same aircraft, weapons, tactics, and, to a large extent, people have been assigned to the Wild Weasel mission. A sequence of upgrades for the electronics provided improvements—most notably the APR-47 Radar Attack and Warning Receiver that is currently state of the art in defense suppression. The U.S. Air Force's Wild Weasels have become the model for other nations, including Israel, that have modified and developed the concept in new ways.

The SEAD Mission

Vietnam introduced the surface-to-air missile and the integrated air defense. The basic lesson of the Vietnam era was that if air strikes were going to succeed, something had to be done about the kind of sophisticated, integrated, multilevel air defenses that the Soviets had designed and built and were supplying to such nations as North Vietnam. The mission was called "suppression of enemy air defenses," or SEAD (pronounced *seed*). It was and remains an essential part of the planning process for the employment of combat aircraft of all types, in all environments, in all parts of the world—in training and in operations like Desert Storm.

The Wild Weasel is only a part of the suppression campaign, and, while it is extremely important, it is only a part of the mission. The EF-111 and EC-130 are both part of the SEAD campaign, but despite what is sometimes written about them, they aren't Wild Weasels. Since there has been some confusion about who and what are actually Wild Weasels, here is a short course in the SEAD triad:

The EF-111 is dedicated to close-in or stand-off jamming; the Raven, as it is called, goes after the data link between the SAM systems. The separate missile batteries will talk to each other via radio, land line, or microwave. They also communicate with the long-range, early-warning detection radars. The EF-111 goes after this communication, effectively blinding the shorter-range tactical radars to threats until they are quite close. This

protects both the Weasels and the strike aircraft from a coordinated, planned defense. This forces the SAM site radars to "come up" earlier and longer than they would otherwise, and that, in turn, makes them targets for the Weasel's Shrikes and HARMs.

The EC-130 Compass Call version of the Lockheed C-130 Hercules is loaded with extremely powerful jammers dedicated to the high-frequency radio spectrum used by enemy headquarters to communicate with tactical units across the battlefield. By isolating the air defense batteries from their headquarters, the EC-130 prevents the enemy units from knowing when strike packages are approaching, their size, altitude, or composition. This also forces the radars to come up, makes their efforts uncoordinated and less effective, and makes them highly vulnerable to the F-4G's weapons and tactics.

Despite the significance of the Wild Weasels, and the publicity they've received over the years, there is still some confusion about just what the Weasel mission is and how it fits into the order of battle. The F-4G Wild Weasel is the lethal part of the triad. The Weasels physically destroy selected radars with missiles or bombs. The Weasel's targets are only those that pose a threat to strike packages, and the current APR-47 system as installed in the F-4G, combined with the HARM, allows the EWO to pick and choose the highest threat to the attackers and to designate it for destruction. As Colonel John ("John Boy") Walton defines it:

"Our mission is strictly that of lethal SEAD; we're the only unit in the United States air forces that doesn't jam, doesn't spoof, doesn't do anything but knock out radars. We can do it with HARMs, Shrikes, Mavericks, or iron bombs. Our preferred weapon is the AGM-88 High-Speed Anti-

This odd couple comes from Spangdahlem, Germany, and the 52nd Tactical Fighter Wing. Normal practice in the Air Force pairs aircraft of the same type. Wild Weasel flights often include other aircraft types because the Phantom's APR-47 system can designate and hand-off targets to the Falcon's HARM missile. USAF photo via Bob Dorr

The EF-111, along with the Compass Call version of the C-130 Hercules provides non-lethal suppression of enemy air defenses by jamming the radar and associated communications systems threatening the strike package. Although sometimes called Wild Weasels, that term is really reserved for the aircraft with the ability to select and destroy targets with bombs and rockets, and currently that aircraft is only the F-4G Phantom.

Radiation Missile because it gives us a longer arm, but we can do it with other ordnance as well. We can accurately detect and locate threats—basically just find them and shoot them. It's a lot like hunting for rattlesnakes: you stir them up so they reveal themselves. But with the AGM-88 you have a ten-foot machete."

One of the most senior Wild Weasels is Lieutenant Colonel Ron Barrett, commander of the 562nd Tactical Fighter Squadron at George Air Force Base. He's responsible for training the pilots and EWOs who operate today's and tomorrow's Wild Weasel aircraft. Lieutenant Colonel Barrett has been in the Weasel community since 1973, has flown all the variants since the F-105, and has a lot to say about the mission:

"The Wild Weasel conducts *lethal* suppression of enemy air defenses—we try to kill the radar! No matter how many times we tell them, people still think Wild Weasels jam the radars. We do not jam the radars, we kill the radars. To do that job, we use a variety of ordnance; the preferred weapon is the High-Speed Anti-Radiation Missile, the HARM AGM-88. It is a very flexible weapon, and with a man in the loop, we can rapidly adjust to changing priorities and changing threats on the ground.

"We also use the AGM-45 Shrike, which like the HARM is an anti-radiation missile. It was developed during the war in Southeast Asia and, despite some upgrades, is still pretty much a first-generation weapon. Its stand-off range remains about the same as it was during the war in Vietnam. And the Shrike is designed so that each model only goes after a limited part of the radar frequency spectrum, so you pretty much have to have one for every different radar. But the HARM covers the whole frequency spectrum.

"We practice bombing SAM sites, the most destructive capability we have. If you can find a SAM site and put bombs on it, you're going to do a lot more damage than with just one anti-radiation missile. However, you're also hanging it out there, to fly right over the top of that guy, because that guy and all his buddies are shooting at you. We did not do that in Desert Storm. We used HARMS, a few Shrikes, and a limited number of AGM-65 Mavericks.

"We're out there to take the radars out, to keep them off the other guys who are dropping pig iron on, for example, a bridge. The Weasels will take out the SAMs defending the bridge so that all the other aircraft can get in and get out safely. And that's what we did in Desert Storm, protecting everything from F-16s to B-52s."

The Navy's version of the lethal SEAD mission is similar, but is called Iron Hand and doesn't use the APR-47 that allows a F-4G Bear to select and choose targets. The Navy uses variants of the E-6 airframe for the job. The Navy also uses Shrikes and HARMs effectively, but differently than do real Wild Weasels.

While each of these SEAD systems is important, the combination of the EF-111, EC-130, and F-4G is much greater than the sum of its parts. Together, they give a theater commander and his planning staff a degree of confidence that strike missions can be launched and recovered with minimum losses. Everybody in the business, especially the commanders, knows that there will be losses. The dreadful days of 1965 and the intense, accurate, effective, coordinated antiaircraft defenses taught an important lesson, the result of which was the SEAD triad and the F-4G Wild Weasel.

To put it all in perspective: the Wild Weasel is just a part of a bigger air campaign, and the air campaign is itself part of a large, coordinated plan of air, ground, and naval forces called AirLand Battle.

Two F-4Gs from Spangdahlem Air Force Base, Germany, cruise above northern Europe's perpetual overcast. USAF photo via Bob Dorr

Chapter 2

Flight of the Phantom

A Personal Perspective

The F-4 Phantom and I sort of grew up together. Although I was designed a bit earlier, the Phantom matured faster, so we took to the air about the same time, and we entered service about the same time, too. As a kid I was interested in all airplanes, particularly military ones. The post-World War II jets were highly attractive, but when the Phantom came along, it was love at first flight.

Previous American fighter aircraft were essentially propeller airframes with jet engines installed—straight wings, slow speeds, short range, and not much more. But the Phantom looked like nothing before (and not much since, either): all angles, huge intakes, and a big radome nose. It's been called ugly, but like a first love, it will always be a special airplane for me. It looks, to me, the way a fighter should look: fast, heavy, with an abundance of muscle if not agility.

The Phantom and I went off to war about the same time, but my combat missions were in slow-movers, helicopters, while the Phantom operated from carriers offshore. The Phantom began proving itself then, back in the middle 1960s, earning a reputation as a full-service airplane that could do almost

anything to almost anybody. It was flying close air support missions for ground units brawling with the Viet Cong and North Vietnamese Army, dropping iron bombs and napalm, and squirting rockets and (later) cannon fire on the opposing team. At the same time, the F-4 was flying air-superiority missions against North Vietnamese Air Force and learning all about MiG-21s, as well as striking strategic targets in North Vietnam. The Phantom played all the roles: ground attack, air superiority, and tactical bomber.

The problem with multirole aircraft is that they usually don't do anything really well, and that was partially true of the Phantom in its debut. The MiG's agility, in combination with the U.S. Air Force rules of engagement and the heavy air defenses over the North, made life difficult for the Phantom. Losses were heavy, kill ratios were low in the air-to-air role. The Phantom could carry huge payloads, but its bulk and mass made close air support an awkward mission.

But the airframe and the aviators turned out to be highly adaptable, and the team learned how to use the Phantom to best advantage.

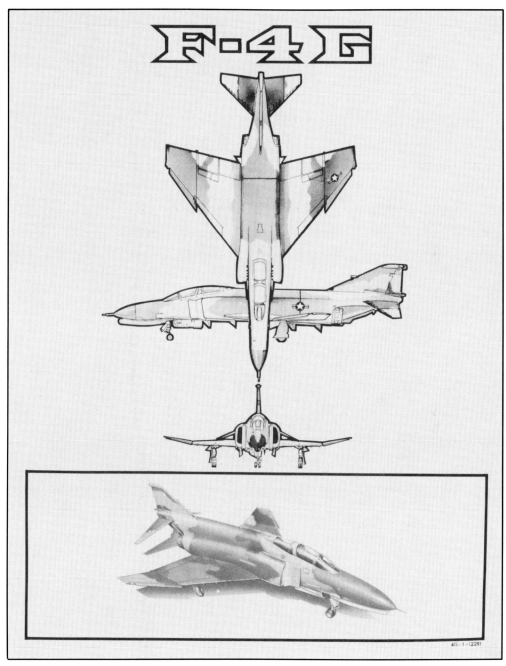

*A page from the F-4G Wild Weasel pilot's
manual, USAF TO-1F-4G-1.*

A pair of F-4G Wild Weasels enter the pattern at George Air Force Base, home of the Wild Weasel until 1992. USAF photo via Bob Dorr

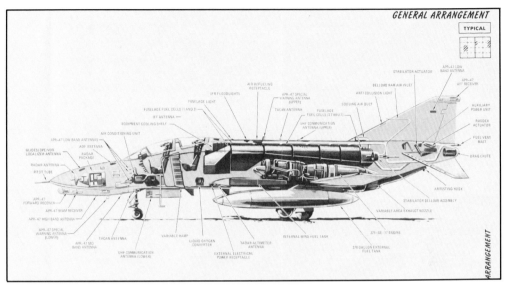

The general arrangement drawing from the F-4G pilot's manual, USAF TO-1F-4G-1.

Phantom Phacts

The basic Phantom was originally designed as a long-range attack airplane for the Navy, based on a specification written in the early 1950s. It first flew in 1958 after many modifications to the original design. By the time it entered service in 1962, though, its mission was to be a long-range, all-weather, fleet-defense fighter. It quickly set new records for combat aircraft performance and outshone its contemporaries.

Much of the Phantom's performance came from a new engine, the General Electric J79; innovations in the design provided tremendous power, redundancy —and a trail of smoke.

Despite the smoke, the Marines and Air Force started buying the Phantom in large numbers, and the airplane began flying a wide variety of missions: air superiority, fleet defense, ground attack, recon, close air support, and the delivery of conventional and nuclear bombs. It had it all, except a gun.

That deficiency was repaired in 1967 when an M61A1 20mm cannon called the Vulcan was incorporated into the design of the F-4E. The E-model was extremely popular, and nearly a thousand were built, many for export sales. It was bigger, badder, and had modified radar, fuel tanks, leading edge slats, and a passenger. Up until this time the U.S. Air Force Phantoms got a pilot and a copilot; now the back seater was a weapon systems officer.

From 1975 to 1981, 116 F-4Es were rebuilt, emerging as F-4Gs. The conversion involved removal of the gun (over the proverbial dead bodies of a number of veteran Weasels) and the installation of the APR-38 Radar Attack and Warning Receiver and over fifty aerials and antennas.

The Phantom, in any configuration, is one of the fastest and most versatile of combat aircraft, even now. It's good for Mach 2.4 on a good day and without external stores. If you don't mind going slower, it will haul eight tons of assorted fireworks into the sky, more than a B-29 Superfortress of World War II. Over 5,000 have been manufactured and have served with at least ten nations as diverse as Israel and Iran, Singapore and Spain.

Operational range is about 2,600 miles for the F-4E, but a realistic combat radius is really only about 1,000 miles. It will climb to about 70,000 feet, then the controls get mushy and you will not want to try going higher.

There are five pylons for carrying weapons, one on the centerline and two on each wing. These hard points will typically accommodate six Sparrow missiles or a combination of four Sparrows and four Sidewinders, or a wide variety of bombs, mines, rockets, missiles, and almost anything else that has standard fourteen-inch lugs on it. This diversity of weaponry is one of the airplane's great virtues, giving it the ability to engage and defeat threats in the air and on the ground, at short ranges or long ones. In the air-to-air mode, even a specialized model like the F-4G Wild Weasel is able to go up against MiGs or Sukhois with some chance of prevailing. As one of the pilots explains, "We've got a long stick and a short stick. The long stick is the AIM-7, good to twenty miles; the latest version of the AIM-9, the 'Mike,' is really a tremen-

The afterburner section of the engine is where raw jet fuel gets dumped, generating lots of noise, flame, and even some more speed.

Using "reheat" or "augmented" thrust is an excellent way to drain all the fuel tanks on the aircraft in very short order.

dous missile. The old version required you to get around behind the guy and shoot him in the butt; the new version works off the heat generated by air friction on the airframe—you can shoot him in the face."

Fighters don't spend much time flying straight and level, but instead squirm around the battlefield. In engagements this squirming can become quite extreme —diving, pulling up, quick reverses. The forces imposed on the aircraft and the crew can be extreme and sometimes dan-

gerous. A human can tolerate about nine times the force of gravity before components begin to suffer damage. Airplanes are typically designed to about the same standard, but when bombs and fuel are aboard it's like a fat guy pulling heavy Gs—something's bound to sag. "When you take off, when you've got all that gas and ordnance aboard, the G limit might be about four, but by the time you land it can be up around eight," a pilot says.

"Other than when we tank, we seldom operate 'straight and level.' We'll go

Mixed doubles are rare in the U.S. Air Force, but here is an F-16C teamed with a G-model Phantom over southern Germany.

high or low level, based on the mission and the threat environment. A European scenario would involve a lot of low-level maneuvering, but [following standard tactics] would mean going to medium level to avoid the triple-A."

That's the combat procedure, but in training there is an emphasis on economy that requires a bit more straight and level than in war time. As one of the EWOs says, "We normally have a single 'bag' center line tank only, and we can go all the way up to the ranges in 'droning mode,' straight and level, getting our best fuel efficiency. Then we go down low level, yanking and banking, for ten to twelve minutes, then come back high altitude again."

A typical training mission is about an hour and ten minutes for only about ten or twelve minutes actually on the range. "That's all we're going to ask of guys to do in a war," says one Weasel instructor, "ten to twelve minutes on station. That's what they did in Kuwait. The low-altitude fuel efficiency of the F-4 is nonexistent, so when you are at low altitude you are pumping 'dinosaurs' out the back end of your airplane! So coming and going we're pretty much straight and level, unless there's an air-to-air threat!"

Even now, the Phantom is a complicated aircraft, which is part of the reason it is no longer in the active Air Force; it is designed in a way that makes mainte-

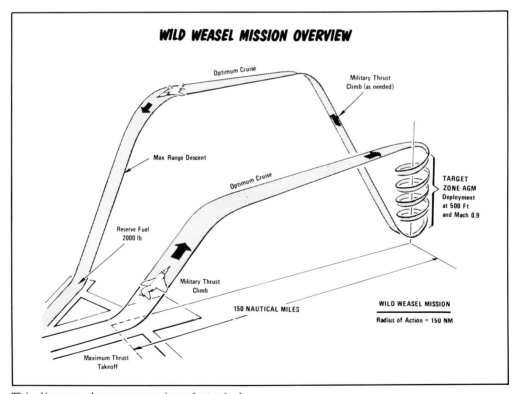

This diagram shows an overview of a typical Wild Weasel mission.

Once you get all comfy in the cockpit, make sure all the cords, clips, and tubes are properly attached; there's still time to wait for the rest of the flight to get its collective act together. Sometimes it can be a long wait.

Besides waiting for the rest of the flight to get its act together, the inertial navigation system has to be allowed time to warm up, and that can take a while. In the meantime, the hot desert sun cooks the crew.

nance and repairs difficult. Newer airplanes have black boxes that are easily removed and replaced, but the Phantom uses an older, hard-wired approach to fabrication.

Flying the Phantom

So you want to try flying the F-4G? No problem, piece of cake; anybody can do it. Well, sort of . . . .

The process of getting a Phantom into the air is a lot easier than you might imagine—in some ways at least. Assum-

It's hard to believe that these beautifully maintained, elegant airframes are older than some of the people who operate them, but most of the Phantoms are about thirty years old. Thanks to the attentions of a horde of skilled maintainers, though, they still look as good as new.

ing that they let you get near one, that you have a flight suit, helmet, oxygen mask, and the assorted qualifications to fly a high-performance aircraft, the Phantom is quite easy to get airborne. But like flying anything well, flying a combat aircraft in a combat environment is an art form.

Flying any military mission involves a ritual that is partly automatic and rote, partly unique, and carefully crafted. Training flights as well as combat operations begin with a briefing and detailed flight planning. The briefing includes the objective of the mission, hazards, communications procedures, routes, emergency procedures, times, IFF codes, and more. In fact a briefing can take longer than a flight, and the whole process of briefing, planning, preflight inspection, and post-mission debriefing generally consume more time than the mission itself.

Then the crews huddle over the charts and plot and scheme and negotiate the details of the flight.

About forty-five minutes before start time you meander down to Life Support to collect your flight gear. The specialists here take care of your helmet and oxygen mask, your "speed jeans," as the G-suit is sometimes called, and your survival kit vest, with its emergency radio, supplies, signal mirror, fishing kit, candy bars, and a little drinking water, just in case. The speed jeans go on here, and the vest too, but the helmet will wait till the last possible moment. The G-suit goes over the flight suit; then comes the harness that will attach to the ejection seat; it is partially donned, but the leg straps are often left loose because it's uncomfortable to walk with them attached and adjusted.

At the appointed time to "step," the crew will hike out to the aircraft if it is nearby; otherwise there will be a van to provide a lift to the parking spot.

Weapons Upload

Well before flight time the ordnance team will arrive with carts of fresh missiles, Shrikes, or HARMs or both. The missiles are equipped with a pair of mounts spaced fourteen inches apart. This spacing is so standard that even MiGs and Sukhois use it, probably a legacy of World War II.

Preflight

Despite the attentions of a crew of highly trained, professional and motivated maintenance troops, the responsibility for the airworthiness of an airplane belongs to the pilot in command. So the pilot in command always takes one long last look at the aircraft before accepting it and climbing into the cockpit. The ritual walk-around inspection begins and ends at the boarding ladder, works clockwise around the aircraft, and is a final opportunity to discover a disaster before it strikes. Tools left in the intakes? Covers or pins or blocks still in place? Leaks? Loose fittings, panels, fasteners? Cracks? Bombs and missiles loose, unfused, misaligned, on the wrong station? Everything that can go wrong will go

There's a good reason for encasing your entire head in a custom fitted helmet with visor down and oxygen mask firmly attached. During an ejection, which can happen on the ground as well as in the air, the air blast imposes tremendous forces on the whole body, particularly the face if it is exposed. Covering it this way provides partial protection, and the oxygen mask helps avoid one of the most sinister dangers to a fighter pilot, the condition known as hypoxia that results when the cockpit pressurization system fails. Your microphone is in the mask, too, so it is normally worn at all times during flight operations.

Yes, there really is an engine in each hole. The pilot is looking for any warped, bent, broken, or missing components, for any evidence of overheat, leaks, residual fuel from the last time the engine was run, or any little hint that the J79 is feeling unwell. Twin General Electric J79s convert old dinosaurs into the speed of heat. The Phantom retains the arresting gear hook that was intended for carrier landings; it still gets used occasionally, even if it is just when the brakes fail and the jet elects to catch a wire at George Air Force Base as a precaution. Preflight inspection involves both a general overview of the condition of the aircraft and a careful look at those things that have been recently installed, especially things that are designed to fall off. Sometimes they fall off when they are not supposed to—an embarrassment to all concerned. These are not baby bombs, but practice ones filled with an explosive charge that leaves a highly visible indicator for the automatic scoring system.

wrong for somebody sooner or later, and the preflight is the last chancc to avoid the ultimate embarrassment—having to abandon an airplane because of a defect that should have been caught on the ground. When you're satisfied that the beast is airworthy, sign the book and start climbing.

You climb about ten feet up the side of the aircraft, using a ladder, and clamber down into the front seat. Connect the quick-release fittings on your harness to the buckles on the ejection seat (a ground crewman will assist). Once secured to the seat and the safety pins are pulled, the Martin-Baker ejection seat can be the best and only real life insurance you can have, on the ground or in the air. The seat portion of the system contains a life raft, survival supplies, water. The back of the seat houses the parachute, the sensors, and mechanisms that automatically separate a pilot from an airplane in distress.

Next, connect the tube from your speed jeans to the outlet on the left side of the console. The G-suit will inflate automatically during maneuvers, applying pressure to your lower abdomen and legs, restricting the flow of blood away from the head and helping to prevent blackout. Protect your head with the helmet, custom fitted to your individual cranium, and attach the left oxygen-mask fastener. The oxygen system doesn't work until the system is energized, so leave the right side off for the moment, but attach it after engine start.

The cockpit is normally pressurized, and theoretically you don't have to wear an oxygen mask. Tom Cruise never had his on in *Top Gun*, and he didn't seem to have any problems with anything. But in the real world where the Phantom flies, you need all the oxygen you can get, especially in combat. And, as sometimes happens, if the pressurization system in the aircraft fails you will become hypoxic, gradually lose your ability to make rational decisions, and sooner or later black out. From time to time pilots succumb to hypoxia and crash. So make sure the mask fits tight, with no leaks, and that you know

Speed jeans look kind of weird. They feel kind of weird, too, but allow you a little extra tolerance of those pesky G forces that take some of the fun out of air combat maneuvering. At high-G loads the jeans are inflated through the tube on the left, compressing the tissue of the lower torso and legs, restricting blood flow away from the head, and keeping you from blacking out at seven Gs; around eight or so you will begin to black out anyway, unless you do this a lot, and then you can stand about nine.

where the regulator EMERGENCY control switch is.

It is okay to fly with the mask unhooked on one side, and it's a lot more comfortable for those hours of transit to and from the combat zone. When you enter a hostile fire zone, though, you depressurize the cockpit and make sure the mask is tight and your visor is down. That's because, if the aircraft is hit, rapid decompression is startling and will fill the cockpit with vapor, blinding you at a moment when you need all the help you can get.

Engine Start

There are two ways to start the engines: one with external power, and the other with your own resources. Normal starts use a mobile generator for the electrical power and air flow needed to bring the engine to life, but it is possible to get things going with the internal battery and an explosive cartridge. We'll use the start cart.

The ground crew will be standing by with the cart when you arrive and will fire up the little turbine engine that provides the air and electricity. A heavy cable plugs into a receptacle below the cockpit, and the pneumatic tube goes into a housing of its own on the lower side of the fuselage, one for the left engine and one for the right.

Normal procedure is to start the right engine first. With the start cart up to speed, turn the engine master switches ON, right engine start switch to START, and signal the ground crew to start the airflow that will spin up the engine. Moni-

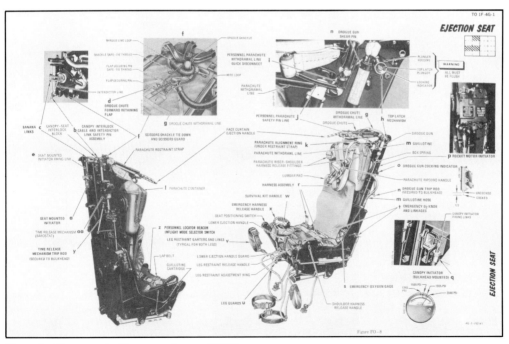

The ejection seat diagram from USAF TO-1F-4G-1.

tor the RPM and, at 10 percent, depress the IGNITION switch and hold it in while advancing the throttle for that engine to about half way, then chop the throttle back to IDLE and monitor fuel flow; it shouldn't drop below 225 pounds per minute.

The air flow will spin the compressor section of the engine, and the lovely rising pitch of a turbine winding up will greet you; then, when the fuel and fire are added to the dense air in the combustion chamber, the engine will light off at about 14 percent with a whoosh, and you can release the ignition button. Now the sound intensifies and acquires a depth and power and life of its own. Engine one is on line; hydraulic pressure is in the green. Monitor exhaust gas temperature for a hot-start,

fuel flow for about 500 pounds per hour. At 45 percent, signal the ground crew to kill the airflow.

Exhaust gas, fuel flow, idle RPM, boost pump, and hydraulic pressure indicators should point to the green part of the dial. Right generator switch is turned to ON, and the warning lights on the Master Caution panel will go dark.

The APU light should be ON; spoiler actuator should work when you deflect the stick about an inch to the left; and the air refueling door and lights get checked for proper function. Start the left engine with the same sequence. With the generators pumping out juice, the BUS TIE OPEN warning light will go out. Signal the ground crew to disconnect the air and

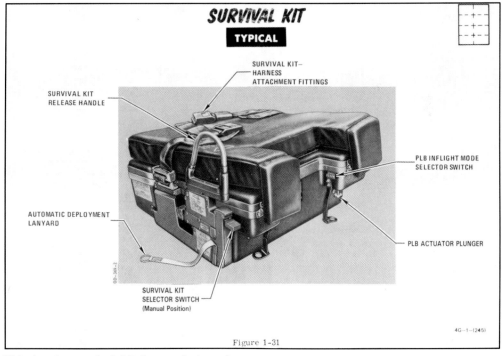

This handy survival kit is attached to the F-4G's ejection seat.

electrical power. You're good to go; no warm up is required, although you should make sure all the little pointers are stabilized before applying max thrust. Check the flight controls, flaps, inertial naviga-

tion system, and radar; then you're ready to taxi.

Call ground control for a taxi clearance, signal the ground crew to pull the chocks and release the brakes, and off you

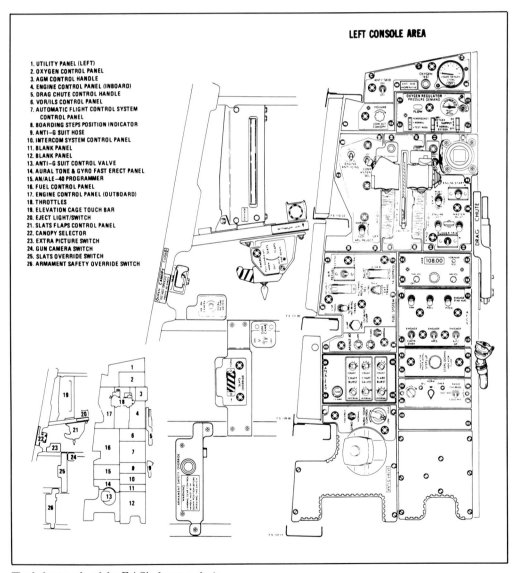

The left console of the F-4G's front cockpit.

go. Test the brakes with a tap on the toe portion of the rudder pedals; engage the nose wheel steering and test with a little deflection left and right. Leave the canopy open for ventilation if you like, and you will certainly like on a hot day—just don't exceed sixty knots.

At the end of the runway you'll get a once-over by the end-of-runway (EOR) crew who'll inspect for leaks, loose panels, and confirm the proper functioning of the flight controls. A separate crew will take care of the arming duties and will pull the pins to arm the weapons. Then you'll get a crisp salute indicating you're ready for the

active; return the salute and release the brakes. It's show time.

Run through the before-takeoff checklist, just to make sure the canopy is closed, flight controls work, there's gas in the tanks, and everything is as it should be. Even old pilots who can recite the list in their sleep still use the checklist, working through it item by item, which is how they get to be old pilots.

By this time you should have listened to the recorded field information on the automatic terminal information system (ATIS) frequency, updated at least once an hour, and made a note of anything signifi-

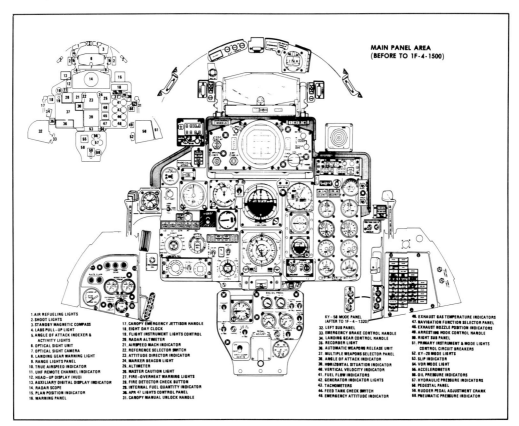

MAIN PANEL AREA
(BEFORE TO 1F-4-1500)

1. AIR REFUELING LIGHTS
2. SHOOT LIGHTS
3. STANDBY MAGNETIC COMPASS
4. LABS PULL-UP LIGHT
5. ANGLE OF ATTACK INDEXER & ACTIVITY LIGHTS
6. OPTICAL SIGHT UNIT
7. OPTICAL SIGHT CAMERA
8. LANDING GEAR WARNING LIGHT
9. RANGE LIGHTS PANEL
10. TRUE AIRSPEED INDICATOR
11. UHF REMOTE CHANNEL INDICATOR
12. HEAD-UP DISPLAY (HUD)
13. AUXILIARY DIGITAL DISPLAY INDICATOR
14. RADAR SCOPE
15. PLAN POSITION INDICATOR
16. WARNING PANEL
17. CANOPY EMERGENCY JETTISON HANDLE
18. EIGHT DAY CLOCK
19. FLIGHT INSTRUMENT LIGHTS CONTROL
20. RADAR ALTIMETER
21. AIRSPEED MACH INDICATOR
22. REFERENCE SELECTOR SWITCH
23. ATTITUDE DIRECTOR INDICATOR
24. MARKER BEACON LIGHT
25. ALTIMETER
26. MASTER CAUTION LIGHT
27. FIRE-OVERHEAT WARNING LIGHTS
28. FIRE DETECTOR CHECK BUTTON
29. INTERNAL FUEL QUANTITY INDICATOR
30. APR 47 LIGHTS CONTROL PANEL
31. CANOPY MANUAL UNLOCK HANDLE

KY-58 MODE PANEL
(AFTER TO 1F-4-1320)
32. LEFT SUB PANEL
33. EMERGENCY BRAKE CONTROL HANDLE
34. LANDING GEAR CONTROL HANDLE
35. RECORDER LIGHT
36. AUTOMATIC WEAPONS RELEASE UNIT
37. MULTIPLE WEAPONS SELECTOR PANEL
38. ANGLE OF ATTACK INDICATOR
39. HORIZONTAL SITUATION INDICATOR
40. VERTICAL VELOCITY INDICATOR
41. FUEL FLOW INDICATORS
42. GENERATOR INDICATOR LIGHTS
43. TACHOMETERS
44. FEED TANK CHECK SWITCH
45. EMERGENCY ATTITUDE INDICATOR
46. EXHAUST GAS TEMPERATURE INDICATORS
47. NAVIGATION FUNCTION SELECTOR PANEL
48. EXHAUST NOZZLE POSITION INDICATORS
49. ARRESTING HOOK CONTROL HANDLE
50. RIGHT SUB PANEL
51. PRIMARY INSTRUMENT & MODE LIGHTS CONTROL CIRCUIT BREAKERS
52. KY-28 MODE LIGHTS
53. SLIP INDICATOR
54. VOR MODE LIGHT
55. ACCELEROMETER
56. OIL PRESSURE INDICATORS
57. HYDRAULIC PRESSURE INDICATORS
58. PEDESTAL LIGHT
59. RUDDER PEDAL ADJUSTMENT CRANK
60. PNEUMATIC PRESSURE INDICATOR

The center console of the F-4G's front cockpit.

cant. At the "hold short" line, switch to the tower frequency and announce that you're ready to depart and that you've copied the ATIS. You should get a prompt clearance.

Release brakes, roll out to the numbers, and line up on the dotted line; apply brakes again.

RIGHT CONSOLE AREA

FRONT COCKPIT

TYPICAL

FRONT COCKPIT

1. MASTER CAUTION RE-SET
2. TACAN CONTROL PANEL
3. CNI EQUIPMENT COOLING RESET BUTTON
4. EMERGENCY VENT HANDLE
5. UTILITY PANEL (RIGHT)
6. DEFOG/FOOT HEAT CONTROL HANDLE
7. COMMUNICATION CONTROL PANEL
8. GENERATOR CONTROL SWITCHES
9. TEMPERATURE CONTROL PANEL
10. IFF CONTROL PANEL
11. DCU-94A BOMB CONTROL-MONITOR PANEL
12. COMPASS CONTROL PANEL
13. EXTERIOR LIGHTS CONTROL PANEL
14. COCKPIT LIGHTS CONTROL PANEL
15. SPACE FOR AVTR
16. COMMUNICATION/OXYGEN LEADS
17. EMERGENCY ATTITUDE LIGHT CONTROL PANEL
18. EMERGENCY FLOODLIGHTS PANEL
19. CIRCUIT BREAKER PANEL
20. FORMATION LIGHTS CONTROL PANEL
21. INSTRUMENT LIGHTS INTENSITY CONTROL PANEL
22. UTILITY LIGHT

The right console of the F-4G's front cockpit.

LEFT CONSOLE AREA

1. INTERCOM CONTROL PANEL
2. CONTROL–MONITOR PANEL
3. RADAR CONTROL PANEL
4. COMMUNICATION CONTROL PANEL
5. ANTI–G SUIT HOSE
6. TACAN CONTROL PANEL
7. MARKER BEACON VOR/ILS AUDIO CONTROL
8. ANTI–G SUIT CONTROL VALVE
9. OXYGEN QUANTITY GAGE
10. CABIN ALTIMETER
11. UTILITY PANEL
12. AN/ALE–40 PROGRAMMER
13. THROTTLES
14. BLANK PANEL
15. EMERGENCY SLATS FLAPS
16. CANOPY CONTROL HANDLE

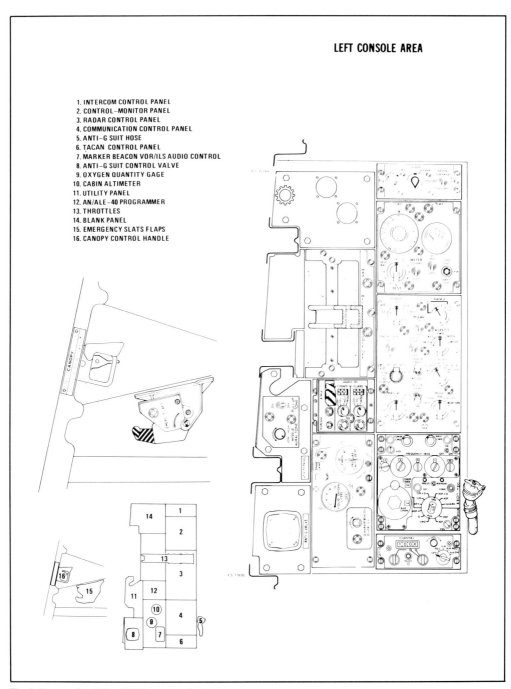

The left console of the F-4G rear cockpit.

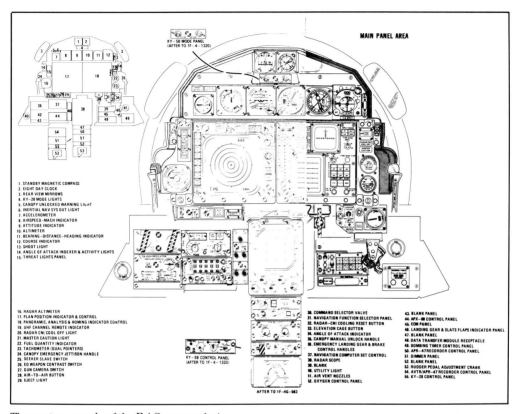

MAIN PANEL AREA

KY–5B MODE PANEL
(AFTER TO 1F–4–1320)

1. STANDBY MAGNETIC COMPASS
2. EIGHT DAY CLOCK
3. REAR VIEW MIRRORS
4. KY–28 MODE LIGHTS
5. CANOPY UNLOCKED WARNING LIGHT
6. INERTIAL NAV SYS OUT LIGHT
7. ACCELEROMETER
8. AIRSPEED–MACH INDICATOR
9. ATTITUDE INDICATOR
10. ALTIMETER
11. BEARING–DISTANCE–HEADING INDICATOR
12. COURSE INDICATOR
13. SHOOT LIGHT
14. ANGLE OF ATTACK INDEXER & ACTIVITY LIGHTS
15. THREAT LIGHTS PANEL

16. RADAR ALTIMETER
17. PLAN POSITION INDICATOR & CONTROL
18. PANORAMIC, ANALYSIS & HOMING INDICATOR CONTROL
19. UHF CHANNEL REMOTE INDICATOR
20. RADAR CNI COOL OFF LIGHT
21. MASTER CAUTION LIGHT
22. FUEL QUANTITY INDICATOR
23. TACHOMETER (DUAL POINTERS)
24. CANOPY EMERGENCY JETTISON HANDLE
25. SEEKER SLAVE SWITCH
26. EO WEAPON CONTRAST SWITCH
27. GUN CAMERA SWITCH
28. AIR–TO–AIR BUTTON
29. EJECT LIGHT

30. COMMAND SELECTOR VALVE
31. NAVIGATION FUNCTION SELECTOR PANEL
32. RADAR–CNI COOLING RESET BUTTON
33. ELEVATION CAGE BUTTON
34. ANGLE OF ATTACK INDICATOR
35. CANOPY MANUAL UNLOCK HANDLE
36. EMERGENCY LANDING GEAR & BRAKE
      CONTROL HANDLES
37. NAVIGATION COMPUTER SET CONTROL
38. RADAR SCOPE
39. BLANK
40. UTILITY LIGHT
41. AIR VENT NOZZLES
42. OXYGEN CONTROL PANEL

43. BLANK PANEL
44. APX–80 CONTROL PANEL
45. ECM PANEL
46. LANDING GEAR & SLATS FLAPS INDICATOR PANEL
47. BLANK PANEL
48. DATA TRANSFER MODULE RECEPTACLE
49. BOMBING TIMER CONTROL PANEL
50. APR–47 RECORDER CONTROL PANEL
51. DIMMER PANEL
52. BLANK PANEL
53. RUDDER PEDAL ADJUSTMENT CRANK
54. AVTR/APR–47 RECORDER CONTROL PANEL
55. KY–28 CONTROL PANEL

KY–5B CONTROL PANEL
(AFTER TO 1F–4–1320)

AFTER TO 1F–4G–503

The center console of the F-4G rear cockpit.

Normal takeoffs are done with leading edge slats extended and flaps down. Advance throttles and run up to eighty-five percent, monitoring instruments for normal response: fuel flow equal to both engines, exhaust gas temp at about 450 degrees, nozzles to one-quarter position, oil pressure at about thirty-five pounds per square inch. Release brakes and advance throttle to full military power. You will feel a firm push as you're accelerated down the runway.

Track the centerline with nosewheel steering (just like you used to do in your kiddie car) until about seventy knots when the rudder starts to provide some authority. With the nose gear still on the concrete bring the stick back; when it's ready, the nose will come up off the concrete. Advance the stick to maintain a pitch angle of about eleven degrees; easy to do if you align the first mark on the attitude indicator. The aircraft will fly itself off the deck with no other effort from you at all.

As soon as you've got a positive rate of climb, get the gear up; when extended over 250 knots the air loads will bend things. The slats and flap controls go to NORM above 180 knots. Maintain the same eleven-degree pitch attitude until 350 knots is indicated; the Mach speed

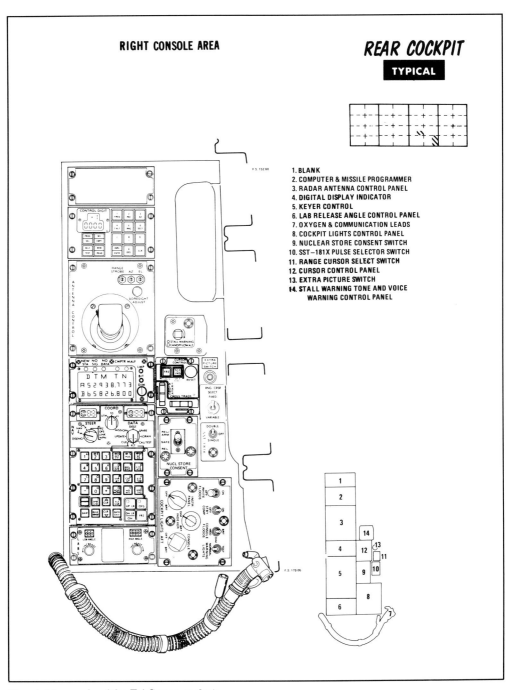

RIGHT CONSOLE AREA

REAR COCKPIT
TYPICAL

1. BLANK
2. COMPUTER & MISSILE PROGRAMMER
3. RADAR ANTENNA CONTROL PANEL
4. DIGITAL DISPLAY INDICATOR
5. KEYER CONTROL
6. LAB RELEASE ANGLE CONTROL PANEL
7. OXYGEN & COMMUNICATION LEADS
8. COCKPIT LIGHTS CONTROL PANEL
9. NUCLEAR STORE CONSENT SWITCH
10. SST−181X PULSE SELECTOR SWITCH
11. RANGE CURSOR SELECT SWITCH
12. CURSOR CONTROL PANEL
13. EXTRA PICTURE SWITCH
14. STALL WARNING TONE AND VOICE
    WARNING CONTROL PANEL

The right console of the F-4G rear cockpit.

will increase to about 0.9, and then vary the pitch angle to maintain that speed until you reach cruising altitude. Pretty simple, isn't it?

Landing

Well, landing is a bit more demanding than takeoff, but once you're up you're going to have to come down sometime. Here's a streamlined version of the right way to do it and live. The process should start while you're still above 10,000 feet and when there aren't a lot of distractions. Again, there's a checklist to follow to ensure that you don't forget something important—like lowering the gear.

The stability augmentation system gets engaged, and the landing light switch turned to LANDING; arming switches for missiles, guns, and bombs to OFF/SAFE; and the altimeters to SET. Check the fuel gauges; the automatic transfer system should make sure you don't suck one tank dry while there's gas in another. Listen to the ATIS again, note significant information, and call the tower for landing instructions.

A normal approach involves entry into the pattern at 300 knots minimum airspeed and an altitude specified by the local authority—1,500 feet above ground level, for example. Fly directly above the active runway to about midfield (or as the tower indicates), then break left to enter the downwind leg of the patter. Roll out, reduce power, and maintain pattern alti-

The start cart has a little jet engine of its own, but if you try to make it go faster than about 5mph on the ramp, you'll get in trouble. The jet engine provides a high volume of compressed air to spin up the engine to start speed. The cart also delivers a large volume of electricity until the generators come on line.

tude; you'll decelerate, and the gear can come down below 250 knots. Extend flaps and slats. Check hydraulic pressure and warning lights; switch anti-skid braking to ON. Maintain 180 knots downwind, then roll onto the base leg, which is one continuous descending turn.

The Phantom offers the pilot some useful cues for bringing the airplane back to earth in one piece. One is a set of tones,

audible in the headset, that indicate approach speed; a continuous tone indicates "on speed," while a slow chirping indicates "too slow," and a faster, higher-pitched chirping indicates "too fast." Use throttle to maintain a continuous tone.

Correct angle of attack is indicated by a set of lights by the head-up display. Keep the light in the middle of the array lit and the on-speed tone constant and the

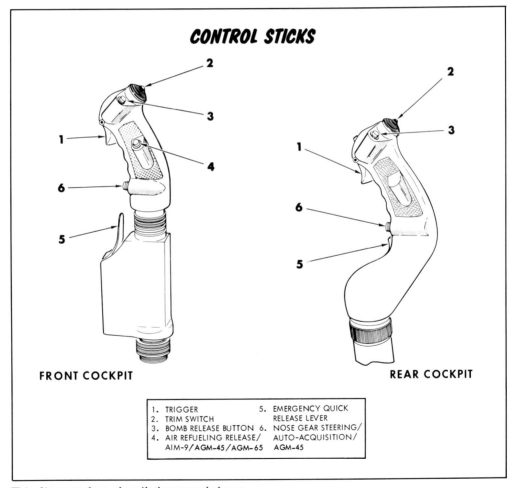

This diagram from the pilot's manual shows the front and rear control sticks.

Phantom will slide back to earth down a two-and-a-half degree glide slope, losing about 700 feet of altitude each minute of descent. If you make sure that the runway is lined up nice and neat in the windscreen, at about twenty feet, ground effect will slow the descent and tend to pitch the nose forward. Maintain the nose high attitude; the wheels will kiss the concrete with a squeal and a puff of smoke from burning rubber.

Bringing the throttle to IDLE, keep the stick aft to use "aero-braking," and pop the drag chute. The rudder will let you steer until the airspeed drops to about seventy knots, by which time the nose wheel with be back on the runway and the nose wheel steering can be used. Turn off the runway, and trundle over to the end-of-runway crew to get inspected and pinned; call ground control for taxi authority and motor back to the parking slot where the crew chief will be waiting. When safely installed at the appointed place, the chocks will be placed behind the wheels and you are free to work through yet another checklist—this one for shutting down the engines and aircraft systems. Wheels CHOCKED; UHF radio OFF; the backseater raises his ejection seat; defog control FULL AFT; temperature control 12 O'CLOCK POSITION; and finally, right throttle OFF, check the spoiler actuator, then left throttle OFF. Engine master switches OFF; APU reject switch NORMAL; all switches OFF; safety pins for the face curtain is INSTALLED; the APR-47 is secured; and the oxygen diluter lever is at 100 percent. That's all there is to it!

"Start Two!" signals the crew chief. He watches for smoke, flames, and flying chunks of metal as the J79 spins up and lights off.

Engine start is a critical activity for a mission because if something is going to go wrong with the engine it probably will be now.

Two F-4G Phantoms return to the roost at George Air Force Base.

EJECTION PROCEDURES

BEFORE EJECTION

A. IF TIME AND CONDITIONS PERMIT
- ALERT OTHER CREWMEMBER
- TIGHTEN LAP BELT
- TIGHTEN SEAT KIT STRAPS
- FULLY INSERT OXYGEN MASK BAYONETS
- LOWER HELMET VISORS
- TIGHTEN CHIN STRAP
- ADJUST SITTING HEIGHT IF NECESSARY
- STOW LOOSE EQUIPMENT
- LOCK SHOULDER HARNESS
- NOTIFY CONTROLLING AGENCY

B. SIT ERECT, BUTTOCKS BACK, SHOULDERS AGAINST PARACHUTE PACK, HEAD ERECT, SPINE STRAIGHT, LEGS EXTENDED AND THIGHS ON SEAT CUSHION.

C. THE FORWARD CREWMEMBER WILL NORMALLY INITIATE EJECTION SEQUENCING, HOWEVER, THE AFT CREWMEMBER MAY INITIATE SINGLE OR DUAL SEQUENCING WHEN REQUIRED. THE CREWMEMBER NOT INITIATING THE EJECTION SHOULD BE ALERTED AND ASSUME THE PROPER BODY POSITION WITH HANDS ON THE HANDLE TO AVOID POSSIBLE INJURY.

1. Ejection Handle - PULL ....

Note

- IF THE CONTROL STICK IN THE REAR COCKPIT IS IN THE FULL AFT POSITION FOR ANY REASON, USE OF THE LOWER EJECTION HANDLE MAY BE RESTRICTED DUE TO INTERFERENCE FROM THE CONTROL STICK. FULL OR NEAR FULL UP SEAT HEIGHT ADJUSTMENT MAY IMPEDE USE OF THE FACE CURTAIN. A COMBINATION OF BOTH THESE CONDITIONS MAY CAUSE DIFFICULTY IN INITIATION OF EJECTION FROM THE REAR COCKPIT.

- ADJUST SEAT SO THAT HELMET IS BELOW THE FACE CURTAIN HANDLES TO ALLOW OPTIMUM BODY POSITION THEREBY MINIMIZING THE POTENTIAL FOR SPINAL INJURY DURING EJECTION.

LOWER HANDLE METHOD   **FACE CURTAIN METHOD**

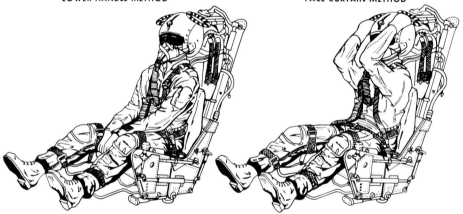

GRASP THE LOWER EJECTION HANDLE USING A TWO HANDED GRIP WITH THE THUMB AND AT LEAST TWO FINGERS OF EACH HAND. PULL STRAIGHT UP ON LOWER HANDLE AND MAINTAIN A CONTINUED PULL. WHEN CANOPY JETTISONS, CONTINUE PULLING UP ON LOWER EJECTION HANDLE UNTIL FULL TRAVEL IS REACHED.

REACH OVERHEAD WITH PALMS AFT KEEPING ELBOWS SHOULDER WIDTH APART. GRASP FACE CURTAIN HANDLE. PULL FORWARD AND DOWN AND MAINTAIN A CONTINUED PULL. WHEN CANOPY JETTISONS, CONTINUE PULLING FACE CURTAIN UNTIL FULL TRAVEL IS REACHED.

WARNING

FAILING TO PULL THE LOWER EJECTION HANDLE STRAIGHT UP CAUSES BINDING WHICH CAN PREVENT THE LOWER EJECTION HANDLE FROM WITHDRAWING FROM ITS LOCKING DETENT.

WARNING

ONCE FACE CURTAIN HAS BEEN UTILIZED, DO NOT RELEASE HANDLE. IF THE HANDLE IS RELEASED IT MAY BECOME ENTANGLED IN THE SEAT DROGUE CHUTE DURING THE EJECTION SEQUENCE.

WARNING

IF OUT–OF–CONTROL AT OR BELOW 10,000 FEET AGL, EJECT.
IN CONTROLLED FLIGHT MINIMUM EJECTION ALTITUDE IS DEPENDENT ON DIVE ANGLE, AIRSPEED AND BANK ANGLE.
RECOMMENDED MINIMUM IN CONTROLLED FLIGHT IS 2000 FEET AGL.

The ejection procedures diagram from USAF TO-1F-4G-1.

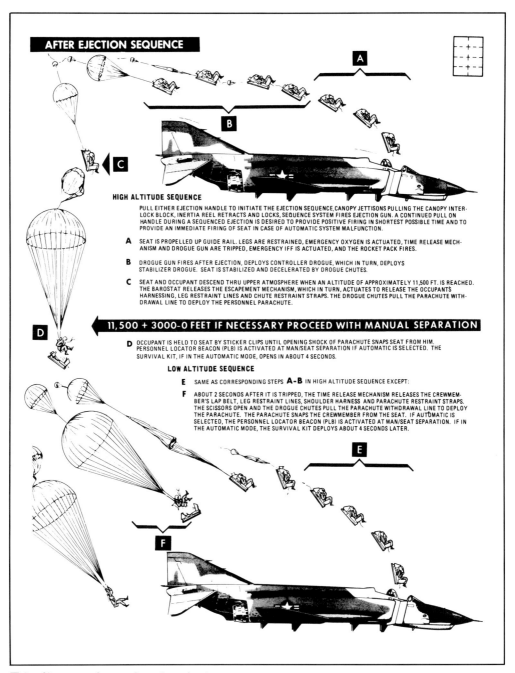

AFTER EJECTION SEQUENCE

A

B

C

HIGH ALTITUDE SEQUENCE

PULL EITHER EJECTION HANDLE TO INITIATE THE EJECTION SEQUENCE, CANOPY JETTISONS PULLING THE CANOPY INTER-LOCK BLOCK, INERTIA REEL RETRACTS AND LOCKS, SEQUENCE SYSTEM FIRES EJECTION GUN. A CONTINUED PULL ON HANDLE DURING A SEQUENCED EJECTION IS DESIRED TO PROVIDE POSITIVE FIRING IN SHORTEST POSSIBLE TIME AND TO PROVIDE AN IMMEDIATE FIRING OF SEAT IN CASE OF AUTOMATIC SYSTEM MALFUNCTION.

A SEAT IS PROPELLED UP GUIDE RAIL. LEGS ARE RESTRAINED, EMERGENCY OXYGEN IS ACTUATED, TIME RELEASE MECH-ANISM AND DROGUE GUN ARE TRIPPED, EMERGENCY IFF IS ACTUATED, AND THE ROCKET PACK FIRES.

B DROGUE GUN FIRES AFTER EJECTION, DEPLOYS CONTROLLER DROGUE, WHICH IN TURN, DEPLOYS STABILIZER DROGUE. SEAT IS STABILIZED AND DECELERATED BY DROGUE CHUTES.

C SEAT AND OCCUPANT DESCEND THRU UPPER ATMOSPHERE WHEN AN ALTITUDE OF APPROXIMATELY 11,500 FT. IS REACHED. THE BAROSTAT RELEASES THE ESCAPEMENT MECHANISM, WHICH IN TURN, ACTUATES TO RELEASE THE OCCUPANTS HARNESSING, LEG RESTRAINT LINES AND CHUTE RESTRAINT STRAPS. THE DROGUE CHUTES PULL THE PARACHUTE WITH-DRAWAL LINE TO DEPLOY THE PERSONNEL PARACHUTE.

D

11,500 + 3000-0 FEET IF NECESSARY PROCEED WITH MANUAL SEPARATION

D OCCUPANT IS HELD TO SEAT BY STICKER CLIPS UNTIL OPENING SHOCK OF PARACHUTE SNAPS SEAT FROM HIM. PERSONNEL LOCATOR BEACON (PLB) IS ACTIVATED AT MAN/SEAT SEPARATION IF AUTOMATIC IS SELECTED. THE SURVIVAL KIT, IF IN THE AUTOMATIC MODE, OPENS IN ABOUT 4 SECONDS.

LOW ALTITUDE SEQUENCE

E SAME AS CORRESPONDING STEPS **A-B** IN HIGH ALTITUDE SEQUENCE EXCEPT:

F ABOUT 2 SECONDS AFTER IT IS TRIPPED, THE TIME RELEASE MECHANISM RELEASES THE CREWMEM-BER'S LAP BELT, LEG RESTRAINT LINES, SHOULDER HARNESS AND PARACHUTE RESTRAINT STRAPS. THE SCISSORS OPEN AND THE DROGUE CHUTES PULL THE PARACHUTE WITHDRAWAL LINE TO DEPLOY THE PARACHUTE. THE PARACHUTE SNAPS THE CREWMEMBER FROM THE SEAT. IF AUTOMATIC IS SELECTED, THE PERSONNEL LOCATOR BEACON (PLB) IS ACTIVATED AT MAN/SEAT SEPARATION. IF IN THE AUTOMATIC MODE, THE SURVIVAL KIT DEPLOYS ABOUT 4 SECONDS LATER.

E

F

This diagram shows the after-ejection sequence from USAF TO-1F-4G-1.

Chapter 3

Into the Pit: Weapons and Tactics

Pilots traditionally get the glory in the fighter airplane business, and the "GIB" (the guy in back) is often ignored by observers, inside and outside of the units. Frontseaters get the Medal of Honor, and the backseater gets the Air Force Cross or Silver Star. Of course, what the pilot tells his buddy in back is that he's merely along for the ride, that anybody could kill a radar with the HARM and the APR-47, and that the backseater has the softest, least stressful job in the Air Force, while he (the pilot) has the real work to do!

Well, the "pit boss" normally has a few snappy comebacks to that: all the pilot has to do is drive around the sky, something the "pitter" thinks he does rather poorly, considering. It is a traditional, friendly, affectionate kidding. Actually, even the most self-confident fighter jock will cheerfully tell you it is a total team effort, that the pitter is the key to success, that the job can't get done by one guy.

The pitter has an interesting job, an interesting place to work. Climb up the long ladder and slide into the backseat, between the intakes. For a big airplane it is kind of a tight squeeze for big guys like Captain Gil Zamora. "There is *no* forward visibility in the G-model at all," he comments. "We call it 'the wall of iron.' In the E models and the 'recces' you could pass notes and see the other guy in the mirrors and know what he was doing, but not in the G. So when you're landing the airplane there's some blind trust there; when I fly in an E model and I look over the pilot's shoulder just to make sure we aren't lined up on a taxiway.

"It's a tight squeeze! You see these big guys—the arms of their flight suits are all worn from rubbing against stuff in there. There's a lot of stuff to get hung up on. But if you don't fit the cockpit, they don't let you start the course!"

The G-model is a different kind of Phantom for the "Bear," or EWO. Its panel is dominated by the APR-47 but includes flight instrumentation, and the GIB gets flight controls to go with them. Every two-seat aircraft in the Air Force has dual controls. Zamora says: "I'm not a pilot and I don't pretend to be one. But I know how to fly the airplane; with 1,700 hours in it, I've flown *a lot*. We typically take over on the long cross-country flights, straight and level at high altitude.

APR-47 Radar Attack and Warning Receiver

The APR-47 is the key system in the Wild Weasel mission. The display is the Plan Position Indicator (PPI). The aircraft's position is the center of the screen, with threats displayed in relative position. Each type of threat has its own symbology: SA-2s, SA-6s, SA-8s, "Gun-Dish," and the rest each getting a characteristic indicator. The APR-47 shows the range and bearing of each threat. It is also programmed to decide which threats are the most dangerous, based on data input before each mission. When you're in the target area and the Wild Weasels are working their beat, this information makes the work of the pitter a lot easier and more effective than it would be otherwise, automating a lot of the chores required to engage targets.

So, the pit boss watches the threats come up on his PPI; they will mostly be

The "wall of iron" is actually made of aluminum alloy and glass, but it still prevents the EWO from seeing where the plane is going. That's just as well, because the backseater really needs to have his nose in the scope looking for the loyal opposition. This is the APR-47, the state-of-the-art in radar warning and attack receivers. The large screen is the Plan Position Indicator, center stage for the Wild Weasel's performance. The buttons on the left of the screen select threat radars by characteristic type.

Captain Espejo waits for his frontseater to complete the preliminaries and climb in to drive the bus. This Phantom is equipped with a relatively rare single-piece windscreen.

expected because the 'intel shop' will have developed and presented most of them during the pre-mission briefing.

Threat radars will normally appear and disappear, only to materialize again. This is the radar operator's way of staying alive for a bit longer. Really good radar operators can drive the pitter nuts.

The pitter will be plotting and scheming, working his art. It requires good judgment to do well. As the airplane advances into the threat area, the pitter has to keep aware of the route the follow-on strike package will take and which threat systems the other aircraft are supposed to attack. Each pitter will have a set of priority targets, and each will have some latitude about which will receive his HARMs.

The APR-47 will automatically select what it believes is the most important target, but the pitter often has other ideas.

He selects the target he wants by moving a designator—a diamond—over the threat symbol. Next, the system accumulates "cuts" on the target, measuring the exact distance and bearing several times. When he decides that the missile's guidance system has enough information to find the radar, he keys the hand-off switch. This downloads the data into the missile's fire control system. In addition to the selected target, the pitter provides the missile with data on alternate targets in the general area. Then, if the primary target shuts off its radar, a secondary target can be engaged. And if they all go down, the missile can coast for a while, waiting for the target to come back up and reveal itself again.

The APR-47 detects radar emissions, but the system is unique because it measures the range to the threat, identifies the kind of radar by its signature, and auto-

Just below the nose of the aircraft are some of the fifty-five threat radar aerials that receive signals for the APR-47. By spreading them out, the system mimics the effect of one huge antenna.

Lieutenant Colonel John ("John Boy") Walton (left) and Lieutenant Colonel Ray Barrett *commanded two squadrons at George Air Force Base when the picture was made.*

Another of the fifty-plus antennas used to receive radar transmissions.

matically prioritizes threats for the aircrew to prosecute. (An F-15 can launch a HARM but it can't select and target the most dangerous radar that threatens a strike package.) The APR-47 lets the back-seater identify, designate, and shoot HARMs at individual radars, and no other aircraft in the American inventory can do that. Not only that, an F-4G can use its APR-47 to designate targets for other aircraft carrying the HARM.

AGM-45 Shrike

The AGM-45 is a first-generation radar-seeking missile on which development began as early as 1958. The missile was built by the Naval Weapons Center; the seeker was manufactured by Texas Instruments, starting in 1963, and the AGM-45 was in service about the time that the Weasel mission was invented in 1965. Each of the Shrike's removable seeker

head assemblies was limited to a single frequency and a single threat radar.

The Shrike is ten feet long, eight inches in diameter, with a fin span of three feet. It weighs 340 pounds. It is a supersonic missile with a range that is probably about twelve miles, but is still classified.

As tactics were developed for the mission, the crews learned how to use the Shrike in ways the developers never intended. A common one was to fire several at long range and at a short interval in the general direction of a suspected threat radar; to get the most out of the motor, the launches were made with the aircraft at an angle of about forty-five degrees to the ground, lofting the Shrike in a high arc. This increased the odds of having a missile overhead when the radars were turned on to take a quick peek at the attacking strike package.

An AGM-45 training missile without a rocket motor or explosive warhead is a safer train- *ing aid than the real thing. The crews work with live missiles as well.*

Twelve models of the missile were manufactured between 1963 and 1981 and a total of over 18,000 were made. It is still in service with both the Air Force and the Navy.

AGM-78 Standard

The AGM-78 Standard is a big missile designed by General Dynamics that began development in 1966 and went to war with the Weasels in 1969. It was something of a hybrid, combining the Navy's Standard surface-to-air missile with a Shrike seeker head. While the missile worked well for the Navy (which calls it the Standard Anti-Radiation Missile, or STARM) it was not popular with Weasel crews despite some advantages over the Shrike. It was, as advertised, good to thirty-five miles—permitting stand-off shots at SAM sites for the first time. And it marked its impact point with colored smoke for the bombers that followed. Its weight and system-integration problems made it difficult to use on the F-105, and the crews generally felt they could do better with Shrikes and cluster bombs. The Standard worked much better on the Phantom later in the war, and after, but was largely pulled from the arsenal in 1987 in favor of the High Speed Anti-Radiation Missile (HARM).

AGM-88 HARM

The HARM evolved from a need for a weapon that had a broad band of frequency reception, inflight tuning, and enough speed to out-shoot the SAM site firing on the Weasel. Development began in 1969 by the Navy and was contracted to Texas Instruments Corporation for production in 1974. First combat use was against Libya in 1986 by Navy and Marine Corps F/A-18s launching at SA-5 radars.

The speed of the missile is another of those little details the Air Force is saving for a later time, but it is very fast, probably faster than Mach 3. It is thirteen feet long

and eight inches in diameter, with a fin span of forty-four inches and a weight of 807 pounds.

The HARM has many virtues, one of the best being its computer memory. The missile can be pre-programmed with anticipated targets—their priorities, types, and locations—and then that information can be changed or fine-tuned in flight. Once launched (normally from about twenty-five miles), the missile streaks toward the target at very high velocities. If

There used to be a Vulcan 20mm cannon under the nose of the F-4E, but in the G-model it was replaced by lots of electronics—to howls of protest from Weasel drivers who wanted to retain a little life insurance for those inevitable close encounters of the air-to-air kind.

the target radar goes off the air (and they usually do) the missile will then look for the second-choice victim; if that goes down, it looks for number three. Once it commits to a target it will close on the victim even if the radar goes off the air, using the best data for targeting. The system certainly doesn't provide a 100-percent kill, but its "kill probability" is far higher than prior systems. The twenty-five mile stand-off distance adds a real advantage over the older Shrike missile that required the crews to mix it up with the SAM sites. About 2,000 HARMs were launched during Operation Desert Storm —including thirty-seven from a single F-4G.

The HARM has undergone the usual evolution of successful weapons systems, being modified in response to threat modifications. The latest models, the AGM-88C-1 and AGM-88C-2, have been upgraded to deal with broader threat spectrums and newer frequency-hopping

radars. The warhead of the most recent will scatter 10,000 tungsten alloy projectiles over a target, some of which will probably hit something important.

As one Weasel backseater said: "The beauty of our system is that we can tell the missile, before it leaves the airplane, *exactly* where the target is, its parametric data, frequency, PRF [pulse repetition frequency], and we can send that to the missile. The missile goes, 'thank you very much,' and now the missile can identify the site extremely easily and select the specific target we want it to kill and ignore the other radars that may be up nearby. It's like 'See that guy? Go kill him!' And if one beam goes down, here's another associated with that site, and here's another; if the first one goes down, use this other beam and follow it down. And if one target goes completely off the air, here are second and third choices in the immediate vicinity."

Taxiing out with a centerline tank and a training missile on the right inboard pylon, a

Weasel prepares to slip the surly bonds of earth.

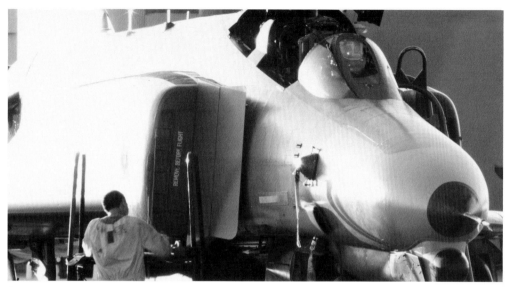

Sunrise out on the ramp will find the unsung heroes of the Air Force, the maintainers, busy preparing aircraft for the attentions of the crews.

Thumbs up; the darn thing actually started.

Chapter 4

Weasel History

Although the Weasel mission used the same basic Hun, Thud, and Phantom airframes as did ground attack, air superiority, and bombing missions, the differences were more than skin deep. The evolutionary sequence started with the slow, unarmored F-100F where the concept was essentially invented. Next came the F-4C, and failure. Then, the F-105F Wild Weasel III, the workhorse of the Vietnam War. During that war the F-4C was again used, in a different and successful configuration called the Wild Weasel IV. And, at the same time the F-105, in its G-model, was flying missions; although tricked out with different equipment than the F-model, it too was known as a Wild Weasel III. In fact there was a lot of overlap of airframes and electronic systems performing Weasel missions during the Vietnam War, and hardly any two airplanes were truly identical within any configuration. There were lots of modifications, tweaks, experimental components in the cockpits and airframes. Weasels have always been oddballs, in and out of the cockpits.

Only three aircraft have been used till now in the true Wild Weasel mission: the F-100F Super Sabre from North American, of which only seven were ever built, the

F-105 (F and G) Thunderchief from Republic and the F-4 (C and G models) Phantom from McDonnell Douglas. In every case the conversion begins with the two-seat trainer version. The process involves gutting the airplane, finding room for several thousand pounds of additional equipment, and then putting all the original components back. With the exception of the removal of the gun from the F-4G conversion, these aircraft are the same that fly the fighter and bomber missions in most exterior respects.

F-100F Super Sabre: Wild Weasel I

As mentioned previously, the first generation was born of desperation with available systems built around the North American Aviation F-100F Super Sabre (called "Hun," short for "hundred"). The F-100 was a very close relative of the old F-86 Sabre of Korean War fame, but not exactly state-of-the-art for 1965—but it was available in large numbers. Of the 2,294 F-100s built, 339 were the two-seat F-model.

The F-100 was, for its day, quite successful and popular; it served in many air forces around the world as an interceptor and ground attack airplane. The Hun was a second-generation jet, only slightly better than the old F-86 from which it evolved. The F-100 was the first US fighter that was truly supersonic, although only at considerable warload penalty. With no weapons on the wings to slow things up the aircraft could do Mach 1.31, about 860 mph. It was propelled by a Pratt & Whitney J57-P-21A turbojet engine that could push it up to 50,000 feet and out to a range of about 1,100 miles. With drop tanks the ferry range was up to about 1,500 miles. The whole airplane was compact and light (by today's standards) and weighed only about 35,000 pounds fully loaded.

It was an interceptor designed in the 1940s—which meant that you used guns, not missiles, as primary weapons when it was first designed. As it evolved, the AIM-9 Sidewinder became an option. The F-model of the jet came equipped with two 20mm cannons with 200 rounds per gun and stations for four Sidewinders. According to the manual you could lash 7,500 pounds of ordnance on the six hardpoints—six Mk 83 1,000-pound bombs plus four AIM-9s, for example (but don't try doing Mach 1.31 with that stuff aboard, or plan on an 1,100-mile range).

The aircraft was selected for several reasons: it was fairly fast, it was available, and it had room to accommodate the prototype black boxes that the engineers were trying to cobble together. And it was cheap, even then, with a unit cost of only about $600,000.

Only seven of the F-model were converted to Weasels, and they were quickly superseded by the F-105 Thunderchief. The F-100 was, essentially, a flying test bed

The Wild Weasel breed evolved from this ancestor, the late, great F-100F Super Sabre—faster than a speeding bullet, but otherwise not quite equal to the task. The mission, as it quickly evolved, required agility as much as speed, and low-level performance as much as long range. Of the first seven F-100s sent to test the concept, two were shot down and all the rest were bent or broken. The mission involved, especially at first, a lot of low-level yanking and banking with rockets and bombs aboard. The airframes got bent by the G forces so much that, in some cases, engines were difficult to change. USAF photo via Bob Dorr

for the systems, tactics and—above all—electronics. This experimental version of the Weasel was what we would call today a "technology demonstrator." None of the pilots or engineers had many illusions that this particular airframe and technology hybrid would be the final answer to the problem, but it was a test bed to see what worked and what didn't. The program was a response to the worst loss rate the U.S. Air Force had suffered since its inception after World War II. Secretary of Defense Harold Brown authorized the release of a special fund of $1 million to develop a response to the SAM threat. Under conditions of great secrecy and with the highest priority, a team of military and industry professionals were given great authority, financial support, six airframes . . . and ninety days to do the job.

In early 1965 the only way to get a line of bearing on a radar emitter was to have a *very* big antenna. There was, at the time, no way to get a sufficiently large antenna airborne so the team came up with a very creative solution: they mimicked the large antenna by attaching several small ones on the F-100. These receivers were installed on the nose, tail, and wing tips. The basic effect of a big antenna was achieved.

When the crews showed up, well into the project, they found the aircraft with their electrical guts hanging out of the access panels and hordes of mostly civilian technicians trying to put them back. It was a chaotic few weeks. The engineers were using anything that they could beg, buy or steal that might make the idea work. Besides the expensive, hand-built systems coming from Applied Technology the components were also coming from the local electronics parts store.

When the dust settled and the guts were all shoved back in the airplanes, three sets of black boxes had been added to the F-100F Wild Weasel I, all the product of some visionaries at Applied Technologies:
- Vector Four Radar Homing and Warning Receiver
- WR300 Missile Launch Detection System
- IR-133 E-Band Multimode Analysis and Homing Receiver

A lot of the success and credit for the program belongs to the civilian contractors at Applied Technologies who developed the system on their own, and to the airframe manufacturers at North American who were expert at integrating systems into the airplane. They all took a lot of risks during the three-month project, and on 21 November 1965, eighty-nine days after the project began, the first four jets took off from Eglin Air Force Base, Florida, bound for steamy Korat, Thailand, with functional systems aboard. Within weeks nearly all were destroyed.

The teething troubles had just begun. One of the problems of the F-100F was that it was teamed with the F-105 Thunderchief in hunter-killer teams. The Thud was much faster, and the old Hun had a hard time keeping up. You could easily overstress the airframe by yanking and banking down low, and in fact many of the Weasels became bent in service. The Hun lacked armor and that contributed to the losses. But when Al Lamb and Jack Donovan finally made their kill on 22 December 1965, the concept was proven. The F-100F first launched the new AGM-45 Shrike in combat on 18 April 1965. Now the system had to be refined. The basic electronics systems functioned so the challenge became one of installing them in a faster package. Back to the drawing board.

F-4C Phantom: Wild Weasel II

The second try at building a Wild Weasel aircraft was another hurry-up effort, this one with the far faster, armored Phantom airframe, using the F-4C as a foundation. To speed things up, the same systems that were used in the F-100F were put in pods and hung on the wings—the "Weasel in a can" or (officially) the Wild Weasel II.

Although the electronics were essentially the same as used in the F-100F test bed, they became much improved, certified, and were renamed. The Wild Weasel II systems included:

- APR-25 Radar Homing and Warning Receiver
- APR-26 Missile Activity and Launch Detector
- ER-142 E-band Multimode Analysis and Homing Receiver
- AGM-45 Shrike Anti-Radiation Missile

The Phantom was an obvious choice for the next Weasel aircraft. It was (and still is) a superb airframe and engine combination that makes the old Super Sabre look like ancient history. The Phantom can weigh in at about 57,000 pounds. It is good for Mach 2.2 (1,450mph) and can be wound up to Mach 2.43 dashes, although not for long. It is powered by twin J79 engines from General Electric. In the ground attack configuration it has a combat radius (internal fuel only) of about 1,000 miles. Service ceiling is up 20,000 feet from the Super Sabre's, to 71,000 feet. The Phantom can carry 16,000 pounds of weapons on five hard points. Two anti-radiation missiles can be carried.

Vibration and transient voltage problems prevented the Wild Weasel equipment from performing even as well as it had in the first generation aircraft, so the Wild Weasel II was never sent into battles. Wild Weasel I proved that the *electronics* worked and that the airframe needed improvement; Wild Weasel II proved that the F-4 *airframe* was equal to the task, but the electronics had to be integrated better.

F-105F Thunderchief: Wild Weasel III

They say that the third time's the charm, and that certainly was the case with the Wild Weasel. When the Weasel in a can didn't work, the designers tried something else: the F-model Thud was adapted and sent to battle, christened the

The third generation Wild Weasel was the F-105 Thunderchief from Fairchild's Repub- *lic division. The Thud was, as one of its crews commented, a real "Cadillac" of an airplane.*

Wild Weasel III. The same proven first-generation electronics were plugged into the fast, armored F-105F, but again the contractors had been busy adding features. The F-105F Weasel III carried the following equipment:

- APR-25 Radar Homing and Warning Receiver
- APR-26 Missile Activity and Launch Detector
- IR-133 E-band Multimode Analysis and Homing Receiver
- AGM-45 Shrike Anti-Radiation Missile

The F-105 Thunderchief first flew in 1955, only a couple of years after the F-100 Super Sabre, but it was a much more capable aircraft. It was designed as a high-speed, long-range strategic strike fighter-bomber. It had an internal bomb bay for its intended weapon, a free-fall nuclear bomb, in addition to wing hard points for conventional ordnance. It tipped the scales at 54,000 pounds fully laden, and was capable of about 1,500mph or Mach 2.25. Its engine was the J75 turbojet from Pratt & Whitney, a strong and reliable performer. Operational range worked out to about 1,800 miles, combat radius about 920 miles. Down on the deck the speed and range numbers were smaller.

The F-105 Thunderchief was built by Fairchild's Republic division; the factory cranked out 833 of them; by the end of the air war over Vietnam more than half had been destroyed. The aircraft had stubby little wings that suited the dive bomber part of its role a lot better than the fighter part; they were so small that the aircraft

Why are these people smiling? Probably because they just shot down four or five American aircraft. For many of the Wild Weasel pilots, the SAM site crews seemed to have personalities all their own, some skillful, others klutzes, all dangerous.

Clip-Wing Thud

One of the incidents that helped establish the F-105's reputation for faithful service occurred when one of the Thud Weasels took a SAM hit west of Hanoi, trimming one wing tip back. The airplane still flew, but with a corkscrew roll that could not be eliminated. The crew pointed the Thud at the coast and said all their prayers as fast as they could remember them. Electrical fires in the fuselage added to the excitement with cockpits full of smoke; with no other real alternative the canopies were jettisoned to clear the air. The flight controls were deteriorating and the coastline was still a blur on the horizon, but the crew decided to stick with the airplane a little longer. Then more flak batteries engaged the aircraft, scoring more hits. But this time, the other wingtip got trimmed and the corkscrew roll stopped. The Thud struggled past the beach to the relative safety of the Gulf of Tonkin, and shed pieces along the way. The crew punched out and the Thud droned a little farther out to sea before it exploded in a massive fireball. The crew was promptly rescued.

Major Merle Dethlefsen won a Medal of Honor.

Pioneer Weasel Mike Gilroy in front of his Thud at Takhli. USAF photo

needed up to 8,000 feet of runway to get airborne on a hot day. It was much loved by its air and ground crews for its simplicity, speed, reliability and tolerance of battle damage. The conventional version of the F-105, mostly the D-models, flew hundreds of thousands of combat sorties. Although slow and vulnerable when all those hard points were loaded, after the ordnance was dropped the F-105 was quicker than the MiG-19s and MiG-21s used by the North Vietnamese, and Thuds killed twenty-nine of them in air-to-air engagements.

The two-seat F-105F was originally intended to be a trainer. Of the 143 F-models built, eighty-six were converted to the Wild Weasel standard. Sixty of these would be converted again in 1968, this time to F-105G format. The first F-105Fs began replacing the surviving Weasel Is in May 1966, and when the Thud Weasel III

An F-105G with an AGM-45 Shrike. USAF photo via Bob Dorr

One- and two-seat Thuds often flew together as hunter-killer teams. USAF photo via Bob Dorr

arrived over North Vietnam in early 1966 the air war suddenly changed.

The electronic systems in the Wild Weasel III were modified in late 1969. The modified system used the same APR-25 Radar Homing and Warning Receiver and the APR-26 Missile Activity and Launch Detector, but the IR-133 E-band Multimode Analysis and Homing Receiver was upgraded to the ER-142 that now worked on the E- and G-bands. The system worked better, but as Lieutenant General Chuck Horner remembers:

"The main problem we had was simply locating the target. We had a system that would measure out the signals, then put a green dot on your gun sight. But the *best* way to get them was to have them shoot at you; when the missile would roar off the pad there would be a big cloud of dust from the booster. Then you could find them *easy*."

In those early days the only way to calculate the range to the target required lowering the nose of the airplane; the APR-25 Radar Homing and Warning Receiver was a "bore sight" sensor that could tell when the emitter was aligned with the nose. With a bearing and slant angle to the emitter a calculation of position was possible—but not easy. Lieutenant General Horner says:

"You were most vulnerable when you were about to launch the Shrike. You had to come in and do 'dip checks,' lowering the nose, then bring it back to level, over and over; the angle between level flight and the angle that centered the needles on the Shrike head measured the range by simple triangulation. But the trouble was, you'd be doing that and you'd look like a monkey bobbing for apples! And of course the guy on the ground is lining up on you! And then, to get added range on the Shrike you had to pull up into a climb and loft the Shrike into the 'basket.' Well, that just put you belly-up to the missile site. So, we had a lot of ways of doing

Captain Mike Gilroy (far right) is congratu- lated on completion of his 100th combat mission by (left to right) Major Merle Deth- lefsen, Lieutenant Colonel Phil Gast, and Colonel Bob Scott. USAF photo

An F-105F Wild Weasel fully loaded. USAF photo via Bob Dorr

This 562nd Squadron bird lifts off from George Air Force Base, tricked out with a pair of AIM-7F missiles, a jamming pod, two HARMs, and a pair of Maverick AGM-65s. The Phantom, never agile, has used most of the *runway to get airborne and is now climbing sluggishly in the general direction of the Nevada ranges. By the time it arrives, with a lot of the gas burned off, it will begin handling better.* USAF photo by Fred Jones via Bob Dorr

business, and it was a bit like the shoot-out at the OK Corral. You had to be a little strange!"

The Thud came with an amazing seventeen hard points for external stores, plus the bomb bay. A total of 13,000 pounds of ordnance could be carried. It incorporated a 20mm cannon, the M-61 Vulcan, with storage for 1,029 rounds, for use against air or ground targets. The F-10FG was sometimes tricked out with the AGM-78 Anti-Radiation Missile, the first that had a memory that could be programmed by the EWO.

F-4C Phantom: Wild Weasel IV

The Thud soldiered on from 1966 to 1969 when the F-4C Phantom became a player on the team, but not a replacement. The Phantom had a whole new set of virtues and vices in the Wild Weasel role, but retained the ALR-25 and ALR-26 systems that had been refined and perfected. To these systems were added an ALR-53 Analysis and Homing Receiver and Az-E1 Precision Homing system for weapons delivery. The Charlie-model Phantom is

An ALE-40 flare and chaff dispenser gets loaded with countermeasure expendables as part of the normal combat routine. Although flares and chaff don't defeat every threat that comes up, they add an important element to the bag of tricks a Weasel crew uses to survive an encounter.

How do you install a very expensive, and very explosive Maverick missile? Very carefully! The ordnance crews are highly trained specialists who can, during wartime, mean the difference between success and failure for combat operations. During the Gulf war these specialists worked around the clock to re-arm the Weasels as soon as they returned from missions, permitting an intense tempo of operations that quickly ground down the opposition.

considered the fourth generation Wild Weasel.

F-4G Phantom: Advanced Wild Weasel

Today's Weasel, the F-4G, is referred to as the Advanced Wild Weasel. It began testing at Hill Air Force Base, Utah, in 1975 and entered service in 1977 with a suite of systems that built on the lessons of Vietnam:
- APR-38 Radar Attack and Warning Receiver
- ALQ-119-12 or ALQ-31 Self-Protection Jammer
- ALE-40 Chaff/Flare Dispenser
- APQ-120 Navigation and Fire Control Radar
- ASQ-91 Weapons Release Computer
- ARN-101 Digital Navigation and Weapons Delivery System

To these detection and delivery systems are added the AGM-88A HARM, and the AGM-78 Standard Anti-Radiation Missile and the AGM-65 Maverick; the Phantom still carries the Shrike as well as the Sparrow and Sidewinder for encounters with airborne threats.

APR-38 Radar Attack and Warning Receiver

The APR-38 "brain" was designed to counter Soviet radars of the middle 1970s. Its foundation was a receiver built by IBM, a Loral display, homing and warning computer from Texas Instruments and a soft-

The APR-47 Radar Attack and Warning System is the heart and soul of the Weasel mission and the F-4G.

ware package from McDonnell Douglas. Four nine-inch antenna arrays and receivers are installed on the vertical stabilizer to provide direction finding. Low-band antennas are installed in the forward portion of the fuselage and on the fin.

APR-47 Radar Attack and Warning Receiver

Instead of a complete redesign, the APR-38 was improved to become today's APR-47 with an expanded computer memory, better antennas and software. Some components of the old APR-38 were combined with a CP-1674 signal processor from Sperry and a directional receiver system from E-Systems. The whole package is still manufactured by IBM and Loral. The result is a system that can deal with a wider frequency range, more complex signals, and more signals in the spectrum—and has far better memory, processing speed, and data handling speed. It is based on a dual-baseline interferometer, a design that provides extreme precision direction finding for radars of many types and frequencies. It acquires emitters at long range, sorts them by type and assigns priorities through an integrated computer. The computer and the weapons are also integrated, making the Bear's job more manageable and a lot less like inspecting sheep guts. That makes the mission of the contemporary Wild Weasel much more tactically important than it used to be. As

The PAVE TACK system adds night navigation and targeting to the old Phantom, along with a lot of extra weight.

Captain Gil Zamora, an instructor on the system says,

"The F-4G Wild Weasel was designed and built to destroy radar directed threats, with the flexibility to react to *real time tactical combat situations*. That's the key to the Wild Weasel mission: if we were just going after the strategic SAMs—the im- mobile SA-2s and SA-3s—we could just send out a four-ship flight of F-16s to drop 'pig iron' on them. But our mission is to go against the *mobile* threats that might not be in the same location an hour or two down the road when strike packages come in."

One of the fifty-five antennas that feed data to the APR-47 is the one on the top of the fin.

Chapter 5

Weasels in the Desert

Warning Order—August 1990

Change of command ceremonies are usually bittersweet occasions, with one officer turning a squadron over to another. It's a time to consider the past and the future, wins and losses, accomplishments and challenges. The flags fly. Wives and honored guests sit in the sun and smile through the speeches. People say nice things about each other, about what's been done and what will be attempted. Then everybody adjourns to the officers' club for refreshments. That's what was happening at George Air Force Base, California, on a steamy August morning in 1990 as Lieutenant Colonel George ("John Boy") Walton was taking over the 561st Tactical Fighter Squadron. The party atmosphere for this change of command, though, is considerably more tense than usual; word has trickled down through the secure channels that a mobilization order is imminent. Lieutenant Colonel Walton has already been notified that his unit will probably be sent to war. "It happened a little quicker than we expected," he says. "We were mobilizing the day after the change of command and we were about ready to go forty-eight hours later."

Although the squadron has labored around the clock to be ready, they are then ordered to stand by. They are ready but there are so many units going to the Persian Gulf that the tankers and reception committees at the destination air fields are in danger of being overwhelmed. So the staff officers and the mobilization plans—after years of training scenarios and "what if" exercises—get a real world mission. A departure schedule is designed and published. The great migration begins.

Launching the Mission

The turn for the 561st arrives on the twelfth of August. The Weasels are airborne, first destination Seymour Johnson Air Force Base in North Carolina for refueling and further orders. They take off again four days later, the sixth unit deployed. The aircraft are configured with travel pods and HARMS, plus AIM-7 Sparrow missiles for self-protection. Nobody knows who might come up to confront the parade of combat aircraft as they cross the Mediterranean, easily in range of Libyan and other potentially hostile forces. The mission is executed as a real world emergency, and the crews are provided a satellite picture of their destination airfield in Bahrain, coordinates for the inertial navigation system and—as one pilot says—"launched into oblivion." The flight is planned at fifteen and a half hours, the longest for an F-4 deployment in the memory of the participants. "It's a long time to sit in one spot!" Lieutenant Colonel Walton says.

Although there is an autopilot, it is rather old and primitive. Its limitations encourage the crews to trade off flight duties, and the backseaters relieve the drivers for much of the long transit. There

The Weasels from George AFB endured a tremendously long ferry flight to the Gulf. USAF photo via Bob Dorr

isn't room to get up and walk around so it gets to be—as Lieutenant Colonel Walton says—a real pain in the butt. The monotony of the trip is broken at fairly frequent intervals with visits to the KC-10 tanker to top off on fuel. The tanker is making the trip in consort with the squadron, a mission the KC-10 crews call a "fighter drag." But the tanker crews get box lunches, bunks, and a lavatory.

The Wild Weasels arrive at an air base, followed by a contingent of C-5 Galaxies. Twenty of the twenty-four Phantoms complete the flight without a hitch, the others arrive shortly thereafter. The 561st Tactical Fighter Squadron aircraft have moved so fast that they've beaten their advance party, who were supposed to arrive well before the fighters in order to have everything ready for the squadron's arrival. The lead element notices that there are only six tire marks on the new runway at the previously unused air base. There aren't even chocks for the wheels of the aircraft, so sandbags are used as substitutes.

The US ambassador is there, and the chief of staff for the air force of Bahrain, as well as a small, glittering welcome party, even if there are no ground personnel to help shut down the aircraft. As the crews dismount and survey their new home they see a beautiful runway, big taxiways, and almost nothing else. It was, they discovered, designed for six or seven hundred people but within a few weeks it held seven thousand Air Force, Army, Navy, and Marine personnel. The temperature was routinely over 100 degrees Fahrenheit, with matching humidity. Living and working conditions are miserable. Arriving personnel are assigned to a space on the concrete hangar floor for a bunk because there is no alternative.

But within a short time prefab buildings start arriving and are promptly assembled. Pay telephones materialize, and pilots and ground crew spend much of their pay on conversations with families. Some spend over $2,000 a month on the calls. Small post exchange facilities are set up, little shopping centers, selling most essentials and some luxuries. A tent city materializes on the desert housing about 1,500 Air Force personnel. They will live in the tents for seven and a half months.

Threats, Intimidation and Training: Operation Desert Shield

Immediately on arrival the squadron begins flying operational sorties; nobody knows if or when Iraq will send armored or airborne spearheads further south. And, if they are going to consolidate their hold on Kuwait, the time to attack is early in the game, while coalition forces are still weak.

The initial mission is to participate in the defense of the forces building up in Saudi Arabia. In the first months, they are tremendously vulnerable. Had they chosen to, the Iraqis could have made Desert Shield a very costly operation. That they didn't probably had something to do with the patrols of combat aircraft that started flying from air fields and carriers in the region.

Three dozen Wild Weasel aircraft join the campaign between 18 August and 5 September. The 4770th Combat Wing sets up shop at Inclirik, Turkey, to cover the Western approaches, with the 35th Tactical Fighter Wing (Provisional) at Shaika Isa. Colonel Ron Karp commands a force now known as Desert Weasel V Special Force with subordinate elements arriving from Spangdalem, Germany—the 81st Tactical Fighter Squadron (Panthers), Lieutenant Colonel Randy Gelwix commanding—and the 561st Tactical Fighter Squadron from George Air Force Base, Lieutenant Colonel George "John Boy" Walton commanding.

For weeks and months the squadrons have been flying training missions that essentially duplicate the probable scenarios of an actual combat operation. This has two advantages: it is good realistic training, and it gets the Iraqis conditioned to a lot of false alarms.

Crewmen load a HARM. Unlike those used in training, these were real "war shots." USAF photo via Bob Dorr

There is also a *lot* of intelligence data being collected. One of the least publicized is the use of the BQM-74C Chukar drones into Iraqi airspace. The drone looks to a radar operator just like a combat aircraft, forcing a response. The response is that every radar system in the area lights up and reveals its position and type—and, usually, a little bit about its operators, too. The Chukars generate a lot of data that goes into the electronic order of battle assessment and the planning for the ultimate opening round of the air war, still days and weeks away.

Before the war starts, call signs are handed out. The F-15s were gasoline brands, Exxon, Chevron, and the like. The Weasels get beer brands: Coors, Lone Star, Michelob, Budweiser.

"Cleared Hot!"—Air War, Part I, Day One

Although it was clear, in those middle days of January 1991, that the fuse was burning, nobody in the units really knew when the explosion would be. So the training continued, people prepared and wondered. In the 561st, a safety meeting was called for 1300 hours on the sixteenth, and since one of the other fighter units had recently lost an aircraft to a training accident, no suspicions were aroused. At the appointed hour the crews gather at "Fort Apache," the revetted compound where the unit's administrative buildings are located. The doors are closed. Personal two-way radios (called "bricks" because of their size) are disabled. The surrounding area is checked for unauthor-

The Weasels began flying operational sorties soon after their arrival. This crew chief checks his bird to ensure that it is ready for anything in case the Iraqis attack Saudi Arabia. USAF photo via Bob Dorr

ized eavesdroppers. General Profit briefs the mission. Colonel Ron Karp comes in and says, "Okay, are you guys ready to go? We're going tonight." He gives a brief talk and sends the crews off for some rest before brief time.

They try to rest, but few achieve actual sleep. Mostly it involves killing time until 2300 hours when the briefing and flight planning begin. "It was probably the strangest eight hours of our lives," said one of the crews, "knowing we were about to embark on something we've trained to do for, sometimes, fifteen or twenty years. It's been a major goal in your life and you wonder if you'll ever get the chance to do it, and now you have eight hours to think about it—that you're going to have a chance to prove yourself, finally."

Lieutenant Colonel Walton briefs that evening, and the flights get about three hours to plan the details of their mission.

Half the unit, twelve aircraft, go to Baghdad, the other half will go to Kuwait. There will be a thousand airplanes scuttling through the skies that night; Lieutenant General Chuck Horner calls it an "aerial ballet" that had to be executed flawlessly the first time—no dress rehearsal. The units had been practicing elements of the mission profile in anticipation of the big show, and the planners had been designing strikes—and then, finally, it was show time.

The deputy commander for maintenance has an idea just before the war kicks off. While the crews are being briefed and mission planning is being completed, he has a big American flag mounted alongside the taxiway near the hold short line at the runway intersection. Work lights are installed. As the Weasels taxi out and off to war, it is the last thing they see on that fateful first night.

The Wild Weasel F-4Gs were fitted with either four AGM-88 HARMs or two HARMs and three external fuel tanks. The tanks were usually necessary because many targets were 1,500 miles away. USAF photo via Bob Dorr

"That was the biggest, brightest, most beautiful thing I've ever seen in my life," says one of them. "It brought tears to my eyes. Nobody knew what the results were going to be that night. We thought we'd do well, but we also thought we'd get some losses. When we saw that we knew there was no turning back. As we taxied out, that flag was the first thing we saw as we headed out for who-knows-what. It was a very emotional evening for all of us." Another says, "I don't think any of us was really prepared for the magnitude of what happened that night; hearing all those voices on the radio and realizing how many airplanes were sharing the sky with us."

After all the waiting and anticipation,

Colonel Ron Karp knocks on the door to the quarters for the news media assigned to the Wild Weasels. They are asleep. He wakes them up with, "Are you guys interested in seeing a war start?" They were.

The Weasels launch a little after midnight.

The launch, when it comes, is just like dozens of others. The flights form up on their tankers, just outside the ground controlled intercept radar ranges of the Iraqis. They refuel from the tankers and then, at the appointed hour, the Weasels lead the hundreds of strikers off to first combat. Navigation lights are secured at the border, and a thousand airplanes converge on Kuwait and Baghdad and other targets in the dark, invisible.

Once the war began, the normal routine was to fly several missions a day, with no more than four or five hours of sleep. Here a Weasel *pilot pre-flights his F-4G before his next mission.* USAF photo via Bob Dorr

When the Weasels returned from a mission, tanks were topped off and fresh missiles were installed in "hot pits" installed along the taxiways—all in less than five minutes. USAF photo via Bob Dorr

Even in times of war the USAF demands that the proper paperwork be completed. Here an F-4G's external fuel tank serves as an impro- vised desk for the filling out of the aircraft's log. USAF photo via Bob Dorr

Care and precision are mandatory when fitting live ordnance such as this HARM. USAF photo via Bob Dorr

The flights break into flights of four in offset-trail formations. Offset-trail makes it much more difficult for the antiaircraft gunners on the ground to predict where targets will be. "We went in as high as we could get," one of the pilots says, "with three bags of gasoline, full-up with weapons, a gross-weight airplane to try to stay away from the triple-A."

Two flights of F-15C Eagles keep the Weasels company, outriggers on the formation. They're along to protect against the "face shooters," the enemy fighters that can launch AA-10 Alamo long range radar missiles and AA-11 Archer missiles with infrared sensors at the invasion fleet. The Eagles search radars help provide an extremely wide coverage against the enemy interceptor threat.

Rules of Engagement

A few of the pilots flew in Vietnam, where the rules of engagement made missions much more dangerous and less effective than many thought they should have been. That was a lesson learned from the past, applied to Desert Storm. This time the gloves were off and the assault would be as intense and overpowering as resources would permit. One of the old pilots, now a commander himself, says, "The rules of engagement we were allowed were *extremely* liberal. It was what we, as fighter pilots, had hoped for: 'Okay guys, if he's a bad guy you are cleared in hot to kill him.' We were given criteria that were extremely simple, easy to understand, and easy to execute to identify an airborne target and to shoot it. So we have this huge gaggle of 'face shooters' charging out there with long-range sticks—the archers attacking in front of the spear carriers—making this wide sweep into Iraq."

Another comment, "We were cleared in hot to engage *any* threat that bothered us, period, dot; we were given a very wide latitude. With the HARM we have the capability to reach out and touch you—or to leave you alone today, and go out and kill this other guy."

The border crossing is invisible except as a way point on the inertial navigation system. For three or four minutes the flight drives into Indian country, then, near a little town south of the Euphrates River, tracers hose the sky. The triple-A is random, unguided, ineffectual. "The tracers really worked to our advantage," said one Weasel. "They showed where the guns were, for one thing. You see those things squirting up into the sky and say to yourself 'Hey, I'm not going over there!' And when they start arcing back down, we would tell that we were too high for them, anyway."

Warloads and Hot Pits

Once the war kicks off the Weasels go off to prowl with either four AGM-88

HARMs or two HARMs and three tanks. The latter configuration is the result of tremendously long ranges to the targets, often a 3,000-mile round trip.

"Hot pits" are installed along the taxiways. As the "Weasel Police" return from one mission they are prepared immediately for the next, fuel tanks topped off and fresh HARMs and Shrikes installed in the revetments. Five minutes after landing the Phantoms are good to go.

Standard procedure for the Weasels is to record each mission on a ³/₄-inch videotape cassette. This provides a record of the HUD information and the intercom audio for later evaluation. This isn't exactly hi-fi audio and video, but it certainly makes for fascinating viewing.

Here is what it sounds like, in a shooting war, when a Stick and a Bear go to work. They are already deep in enemy territory and already have their target selected.

"Looking good up here; the scope is clear, except for his [target] radar on it."

"Target's set."

"Thank you! I've got it at twenty-five miles, 040—and he's gone 'light's out' on me."

"Go to twenty-five–mile scope. Target's on the beam, twenty miles."

"Start a right turn."

"Okay, coming to the right."

"Target coming on the nose—fifteen miles!"

"Roger that; fifteen miles on the nose."

"In about three miles, start your turn to the left."

"Two bar, twelve miles. Okay, two bar is dotted . . . we're coming into their airspace. . . ."

A fully loaded F-4G Phantom waits on the line for its Electronic Warfare Officer (EWO) to mount up. The EWO uses the APR-47 Radar Attack and Warning Receiver to find and attack enemy SAM sites. USAF *photo via Bob Dorr*

The flight line of the Wild Weasel base at Shaika Isa was a busy spot, with Weasel aircraft landing and launching at all hours.

Here the ground crews prepare a flight of four F-4G's for launch. USAF photo via Bob Dorr

Off on another mission, a Wild Weasel Phantom launches from its base. During Operation Desert Storm, most bases housed a wide *variety of aircraft, such as the Marine Intruders in the foreground.* USAF photo via Bob Dorr

"Boy, they're shooting like crazy down there!"

"Roger that. The three's back dotted; got an 'eight' [SA-8 SAM] up! We need to get away from the target! We're at ten miles."

"Coming right!"

"Target now at four o'clock, fifteen miles. Range quality two. Okay, let's turn and shoot this guy! Roll out here, we'll take a beam shot."

"I'm rolling out."

"Target hand-off [the APR-47 sends the precise targeting data to the missile seeker]. Ready light!"

"Shoot him!"

"Missile away!"

"Okay, we've got range quality one on the 'three' [SA-3 SAM]. Turn to the right!"

"Coming right."

"He's up. He's dotted. Keep your turn coming. Target hand-off!"

"Rolling out!"

"Ready light!"

"Shoot him!"

"Missile away!"

"Is he up?"

"No—yes, he's up! Come up and die!"

"Coming right."

"Got an optical launch on the 'two' [SA-2 SAM]."

"Coming right. Let's have some chaff."

"Okay. Triple-A on the right side. Chaff coming out. Got a big flash on the left!"

"Let's get out of here."

"Okay! I think we've done our share for king and country."

Both launches are later confirmed as kills.

Getting Into the Routine

The initial attack is intended to be devastating, and it is. For the Weasel Police it means a relentless pace for the crews in the air and the crews on the ground. The normal routine involves several missions a day, with no more than four or five hours of sleep.

Later, as the unit settles into a sustainable routine, Lieutenant Colonel John Walton tries to ensure the crews have ten or twelve hours on the ground. The crews object, though. "They were complaining that they weren't getting their fair share of sorties!," Lieutenant Colonel Walton says.

The Weasel Police are always into the target area ahead of the rest of the strike package. In the words of one Weasel: "We like to get in there at least a few minutes early to gather data on the enemy 'electronic order of battle' so we can selectively target the threats against the strikers. The longer we're in there, the more accurate we are. Ideally, that's three to five minutes from the leading edge of the strikers—although, because of the distance to some of the targets, we were occasionally limited to just a minute or two."

Once the war kicks off the electronic intelligence collection goes into high gear. One of the Weasel pilots explains, "You've got a lot of collectors up there, gathering information at first. They're watching how the enemy emitters are reacting to us, how their systems are working, what they're doing. Then, the follow-on missions go 'Okay, these guys were the ones who were driving the fight yesterday. Let's kill those guys today so they won't be able to drive the fight tomorrow.'

"We started out the war trying to be very 'comm' [radio communications] limited, but as it turned out, nobody was talking much so we went to a low-comm regime. So everybody knew pretty early on who the beers [Wild Weasels] were, and nothing could make me prouder than to hear on frequency 'Are there any beers airborne?' Meaning, 'Have we got Weasels up there so we don't have to worry about getting shot at.' In fact some of the B-52s were slow to cross the border unless Weasels were on station."

Going Downtown

Baghdad is still just a glow on the horizon. Triple-A comes up ineffectively, other than to keep the adrenaline flowing. Then the APR-47 starts to earn its keep. As the SAM radars come up, each is identified by type, range, and bearing. SA-2s, SA-3s, SA-6s appear, blossoming on the screens. "It was so thick with threats you didn't want to look at it," an EWO reports. "It was a classic 'target-rich environment.' So our job was to go after the highest priority threats, which we determined by looking at type and geographical location."

The Weasels try to get as close as possible to the targets while still staying outside the SAM threat envelope. Since HARMs can be launched at beam threats or even at targets astern, targets are engaged in ways that make it most difficult for the ground threats to kill the Weasels while increasing the probability of hit for the HARMs. One of the best ways they use is to approach targets indirectly, keeping them off to the side. This makes it far more difficult for the radars to track the airplanes while still keeping the SAM sites easily inside the AGM-88 HARM's range.

Nearby, and part of the strike package, are the EF-111 Ravens. They are the tactical jammers, contributing to the force mix by blinding some of the radars rather than killing them. It's an effective technique, even if temporary, but the Ravens need protection. They set up a taco-shaped orbit off to one side of the air-borne battlefield, with a small posse of F-15Cs for company, and go to work.

Shark-mouthed F-4Gs taxi out with three "bags" of gas. The tanks each carry 370 gallons of fuel. Even with all this extra fuel the

Weasels required tanker support for missions deep into Iraq. USAF photo via Bob Dorr

In the target area, particularly at the beginning of the fight, the threat from Iraq's Mirages, MiG-29s, and other fighters is high. The Weasel Police have to concentrate on the primary mission while listening for calls from the AWACS and fighter screen. But the concentration level is high enough that most of the threats are quickly ignored. As one of the EWOs says, "A lot of times you don't give the air-to-air threat as much attention as you'd like. I listened to one of our mission tapes and the Eagles were calling out where the 'bandits' were—but I don't remember hearing *any* of it. I think your 'brain processor' quickly determines if that guy is going to be a threat to you in the next minute or so and then ignores it if he's not

. . . because in another minute you might not even be alive."

The Weasel flight drives on into Baghdad, leading the parade. Even though their navigation lights are out, they're painting each other on radar and have a good idea of the disposition of the squadron aircraft. "About this time we start seeing *a lot* of radar systems coming up," said the EWO. "I had two HARMs on board, and two priority targets, plus secondary and tertiary targets if my primaries weren't up. Our job was to clear lanes for the follow-on flights of strikers, give them safer avenues of attack. Our job was to blow these guys out so the strike packages could move through."

The ageing F-4G proved its worth again in the Gulf. Phantom 69-7263 shot thirty-seven HARMs at Iraqi targets. Phantom 69-7231 flew forty-seven missions and 155 combat hours. USAF photo via Bob Dorr

The first three aircraft have specific targets to engage. Number four bats "cleanup," and will take out targets of opportunity that might not have been available to the first ships in the flight. A tactic of the enemy systems operators is to operate intermittently, for brief periods, to defeat the Weasels, so the possibility of a particular aircraft being able to engage its primary target is often slight. But the radars have to come on sooner or later if they are to be effective at all, so all of the crews are flexible about the exact targets they engage. "In our four-ship," said one Weasel, "the number four guy knows number one and number two is supposed to kill *this* target, and *that* target, he knows the time-of-flight for the missile. He watches and says to himself, 'Okay, here are our priority targets. This one didn't die yet. I'll kill him. This other one hasn't died yet, either, so I'll kill *him.*' And behind that flight are eight other Weasels doing essentially the same thing."

Attriting the Enemy

The process is gradual, abrasive, a kind of art form. The lead elements have the comparatively easy task of engaging their primary targets, but the follow on flights have to react, to work down the list of alternates. One by one the threat systems go away.

"At this point," said another Weasel, "the Iraqis didn't have a clue what was going on—what we call a 'Profile Three' tactical situation. They basically threw the switch to turn on the system—and left it on! The EF-111s, the Compass Call, the strikes that went in as we crossed the border against their GCI sites all worked. They were deaf, dumb, and blind at this point, the initial shock of battle. They went to their systems, turned them on and started looking for targets. We knew, based on intel reports, that their SAMs couldn't hurt us. So when they came up, they did exactly what we wanted them to do!

"We forced them into an autonomous operation. We wanted them to stay on for as long as possible. Our APR-47 system was able to go cut, cut, cut—boom! I know your *exact* location now, I can 'step' to you, target you, shoot you. The missile has the full time of flight to hit it, and the system stayed on for the full time of flight, giving the missile its highest probability of kill."

Teamwork and Tactics

Lieutenant Colonel Ron Barrett describes how he and his Bear sorted out crew duties:

"My 'pitter' and I agreed that my head was going to be outside, watching what's going on, his head was going to be inside looking at the electronics. The way the F-4's intakes are positioned he can't see what's below us much anyway—so I've got my 'Mk 1 Eyeball' looking all over the place for threats. The backseater is looking at his APR-47 scope, watching as the radar threats come up, saying, 'okay, that's John-Boy's and Bud Redmond's there, Nat's and Buster's targets are up over here, my target's up over here . . .' So my 'pit boss' is looking at all those threats, and he's letting the APR-47 do its thing—figuring out where the targets are, based on the ELINT [electronic intelligence]. Then he says, 'I got enough to kill these guys, to shoot with an extremely high probability of kill.' The pitter is telling me what our range quality is, our time, how we're doing, location, what the other guys are doing around us. He's keeping me informed, maintaining my situational awareness. I'm not saying much to him at all.

"It turned out to be very businesslike, probably because we'd done it so much.

Everything we had done before led up to this. From day one they start teaching you to work as a team. And we are so standardized now that it is taken for granted who does what to whom. Add to that the fact that we had been flying with the same guy for at least two or three months. We got to know each other so well that, with just one or two words in the cockpit we were able to communicate volumes."

As all combat veterans know, there are some aspects of the combat experience training that never really duplicate. The most important one of these is the tangible effect being under actual hostile fire has on people and their performance. In training there is always the expectation that you can push on a little more to collect a little extra data to fine tune a shot. Not so in combat, as in the attack described in this exchange between one pilot (Major Dan "Scruffy" Ruffin) and his backseater (Captain Jim "Casper" Avrit) on the first night over Baghdad.

Pilot: "Okay, we need to shoot."

EWO: "A little closer."

Pilot: "We need to shoot!"

EWO: "I need one more cut to sweeten the shot."

Pilot: "Jim . . . they are *shooting* at us!"

EWO: "Oh, really? Hand-off! Ready light! Magnum!" as the missile comes off the rails.

The APR-47 and HARM in Combat

Target hand-off sends fresh data acquired by the APR-47 and selected by the EWO into the computer memory of the HARM, providing highly specific and accurate information that the missile can use to home on the threat radar. The hand-off button is just to the side of the APR-47 display; push it and there is a momentary delay, then the ready light illuminates

indicating the missile is loaded and good to go. When the pitter calls "Target hand-off," the pilot keeps the aircraft stable for a few seconds to give the missile its maximum probability of a kill. The pitter calls "Ready light! Magnum!" and pushes the pickle switch on his control column grip. The pilot now knows the missile is about to come off the station he has previously selected; he has also armed the system with the MASTER ARM control—it is the frontseater's call if anything comes off the airplane. He must consent to fire. Pilots generally appreciate knowing when the missile is about to come off the rails, for several reasons: "Tell me when you're going to shoot the thing so I'm not looking at it and ruin my night vision," says one, "and so it doesn't scare the hell out of me! Once he didn't over Kuwait, and it scared the *piss* out of me! I thought something had blown up right next to the airplane."

Almost none of the crews had ever fired a HARM before launching one in combat.

"Check thirty left. Hand-off! Ready light! Magnum!" The HARM comes off with a loud whoosh, a flash, and leaves very, very fast, a sudden flood of white light that rapidly shrinks to a small dot streaking away toward the unseen target below. The EWO "K-marks" that target on the APR-47, indicating that it has been engaged, but the crew don't pay much more attention to it now. The pilot comes back to his base course, the next missile is now selected and the EWO watches for built-in test (BIT) error lights; it checks good, the pit boss selects the next target. With good data he calls "check thirty left" again, then "Ready light! Magnum!" Both HARMs are often fired within the space of a minute.

After the first few missions the crews come off the adrenaline a little and settle into a routine. Some even start whining about not getting as many missions as they'd like. HARMS, which had previously been far too precious to launch, now are evaporating from the inventory at a rapid rate. Ground crews and air crews, planning staff, and logistical support folks finally start using all the months, years, and, in some cases, decades of training in a shooting war. Confidence builds as everybody discovers that the systems and tactics actually perform as advertised. It is a very exciting and satisfying experience for nearly everybody.

The ground campaign kicks off—and suddenly, it is over.

The average mission worked out to be a bit over four hours long. The 561st Tactical Fighter Squadron flew 1,176 sorties in the campaign. Virtually all the crew members log at least 100 combat hours in the forty-two–day war. Each ten combat sorties qualified a crew member for an Air Medal.

"The good news," Lieutenant Colonel John Walton says, "is that we brought them all home, too."

Chapter 6

Son of Wild Weasel: The Future

The original Wild Weasel, the old F-100F with its Vector Four Radar Homing and Warning System, only survived a few months and has long since retired. But a sequence of descendants have perpetuated the breed, the F-4G being only the current configuration. The F-105F and F-105G version served for more than twenty years, finally retiring in the Air National Guard only in 1987. Now it is the Phantom's turn to stand down. It will serve out another few years with the Air National Guard, too, before a last flight to the bone yard at Davis Monthan Air Force Base in Arizona, one of the saddest places on earth for people who love airplanes. A lucky few airframes will be dissected and embalmed, repainted and put on a pedestal or parked in some museum display. But most will simply rot in the Arizona sun. But the Phantom, despite its age and wrinkles, will remain a beloved system for many years; as Captain Gil Zamora says, "Every weapon the air force has ever put on an airplane has been proven on an F-4 —all the air to air missiles, all the air to ground missiles, nukes, and now defense suppression. The F-4 has done it all!"

But Lieutenant Colonel Ron Barrett has a squadron commander's perspective on the aircraft: "The cost of an opera-tional squadron of F-4s is probably about the same as several F-16 squadrons, maybe an entire wing! That's because of logistics and maintenance. The airplane's old. The black box theory doesn't work in an F-4. To trouble shoot a hydraulic leak in an F-4 takes *days*. Any airplane, if it's maintained properly, can keep flying in-definitely. With an F-16, if you've got a problem you just pull out a box, put in a box. You take the broken box back to the shop and fix it there. With this airplane there is a lot of stuff you've got to work on while it's on the airplane."

Some of the airframes are so old that they've been flown by two generations of Air Force pilots, father and son, twenty years apart. There's something nice about that, I think: that a system works so well that it is maintained for many years in spite of newer technologies and styles of aircraft design.

Despite the F-4Gs obvious capa-bilities, the Air Force decided in 1990 to retire the aircraft from active duty. There were several reasons, all good: (1) it's an old airframe, with systems that are diffi-cult and expensive to maintain; (2) it's an airframe dedicated to one mission and one mission only, unlike more contempo-rary aircraft which can perform multiple roles as required; (3) its mission can be performed by other—perhaps even new —airframes which are easier and cheaper to maintain.

So, in an Air Force and a military community that was shrinking rapidly, the Phantom just didn't fit anymore. The last classes were scheduled at the 562nd Tactical Fighter Training Squadron at George Air Force Base in California—a base that was planned to be closed down in 1992. The last pilots would be from the Idaho Air National Guard; they would fly the Phantom for another five or ten years, then it would be gone forever.

But then came Operation Desert Storm and the most intensive and sophisticated air defenses outside of the Soviet Union.

As Desert Storm concluded, the old Phantom was at the apogee of its development, its capability, and its contribution to battle, and supposed to be retired from active duty. But, on further reflection, the F-4G will continue to serve until a G-model F-15 or F-16 is developed to replace it. They will be flown until the late 1990s, when their airframes will have fnally completed their service life, to be retired to museums or beer cans. For the Air Force it has become simply a matter of money. The Phantoms have become just too expensive to keep in service, no matter how well their systems may perform in the air. So alternative Wild Weasel systems and strategies are being designed and tested. And until they are ready, the Phantom and the Air National Guard will be ready for a crisis.

U.S. Air Force aircraft wear a lot of information on their tails: the Tactical Air Command shield, for the units' parent command; WW for George Air Force base, home of the Wild Weasel; 69 for the year the airframe was constructed; and 305 for the airframe number. The stripe is actually a low-intensity light source for formation flight at night.

Follow-On Wild Weasel

The Phantom's replacement is referred to as the Follow-On Wild Weasel, and is supposed to have a new airframe, new multipurpose receiver, coupled with the old Shrike, HARM, and a new low-cost, high-speed medium-range anti-radiation missile. There has been considerable debate about which airframe will be assigned the mission. It may be a F-15E Strike Eagle or the F-16, modified to accept the APR-47. That hasn't (at this writing) been decided. These aircraft may be dedicated Wild Weasels or may be conventional aircraft within a regular fighter squadron who fly defense suppression missions while the rest of the aircraft execute the strike mission. While no one thinks such a plan would result in a system as marvelously capable as the Phantom and its dedicated Weasel drivers, everyone thinks it will be less expensive.

The key issue for the Air Force is cost; the new airframes can handle perhaps eighty percent of the F-4G's functions, but at a far lower cost. And all 200 F-15Es will be modified to be able to launch HARMs, even though they won't have the APR-47 to prioritize and designate targets with the discrimination of the old system.

Many Phantom drivers and EWOs aren't convinced this is such a hot idea. It seems like a step backwards, in some respects, to surrender the APR-47 in order to get a less expensive platform to launch HARMs. Captain Gil Zamora says, "Just because you hang a HARM on an F-16 or F-15 doesn't make it a Weasel. Nobody has the detection capability that we have.

Every time the pilots go off to play for an hour or two, a team of support and maintenance people spend about twenty hours cleaning up after them. Here's one of them putting the laundry away—a freshly packed braking parachute going back into its container. Just about the time they get all the bugs off the windshield, those pesky pilots will want to take the plane out again. Oh well.

They'll have to shoot three or four to do what we do with one."

"We certainly could use a new airframe," Lieutenant Colonel Ron Barrett says. "There are good candidates out there: the F-15E would be a *great* candidate; it can carry lots of ordnance, it's already a two-place airplane, it's got all kinds of sensors that can integrate with our SAM finding equipment—but I don't think it's going to happen any time soon."

The reason it won't likely happen soon is that it costs lots of money. Instead

Despite what the other books say, not all Phantoms have folding wings. The Es and Gs traded that feature for leading edge slats, seen here in the retracted position. Slats improve slow-speed handling and are automatically scheduled through the pilot's FLAP/SLAT control and the flight control computer.

The Phantom driver's view is hardly better than the GIB's, but at least he can see a little of the terrain ahead of the aircraft. And that's a good thing, too, because the aircraft will be down close to it during tactical operations.

"Are you sure *this thing is airworthy?" A crew confers with the crew chief for one of the* G-model Phantoms before climbing aboard for an hour's frolic over the Nevada ranges.

Chapter 6

Cluster bombs are sheet metal cans with large numbers of submunitions inside. At a predetermined altitude over the target, a strip of explosive cord "can-opener" releases the little bomblets, dispersing them across a target and, hopefully, sending the radar (and the operator) back to the repair facility.

of tricking out the F-15 with the APR-47, an alternative being considered is to give the F-16 some of the capability of the Weasel —but not all. Of course, the Falcon can shoot HARMs now, although it can't designate with the precision of a Phantom.

An alternative is to make the Weasel mission a component of a squadron's duties, along with the air superiority and attack roles. An F-16 unit might have a third of its aircraft tricked out to do defense suppression—perhaps in addition to other duties. As Lieutenant Colonel Barrett says, "The beauty of the Wild Weasel today is that you can go out there, look at the whole electronic order of battle, see which radars are up, see which ones pose a threat to the strikers and *surgically* remove those threats. That's quite different from some of the ideas being proposed as replacements— airplanes without the capabilities of the F-4G Wild Weasel can go out there and shoot a HARM but it's like throwing darts in the dark. You're going to hit something, but you don't know what it will be."

So what breed of Weasel is the US Air Force likely to acquire? That's still up in the air, as of this writing. But Lieutenant General Chuck Horner has probably been thinking about the problem as much as anybody in the decision-making loop.

"Before Desert Storm we were planning on getting rid of the Weasels," said Horner. "They are an old airplane, and people thought we could get by with what some people call a "dumb" Shrike or HARM shooter—an aircraft that just shoots one out there without really picking the signal, and lets the missile select the target. But I always thought that if we were doing a selective operation— evacuating people from a small country during a revolution, for example—it would be very nice to have a selective shooter that could sit over the airport our C-141s are going into and who would know not to shoot at the 'friendlies' and could pick out the signals of the unfriendlies.

"And, then during Desert Storm the Weasels became the favorite of the fighter and bomber pilots. They were more concerned with how the Weasel Police were doing than almost anything else. They really appreciated the destructive aspects of the SEAD mission and really appreciated what the Weasels did for them.

"We used a lot of lessons we learned in Vietnam, and made sure we didn't repeat the mistakes we made there."

Index